Digital Marketing in 2017

DAVID BAIN

ISBN: 1540729990
ISBN-13: 978-1540729996

WHAT OTHERS ARE SAYING

"I'm very impressed that David managed to pull this off! Interviewing over 100 digital marketing experts in one show was an absolutely epic undertaking and this book pulls together everyone's thoughts in a well-categorised and actionable format. If you're looking for an easy-to-follow overview of the most important digital marketing tactics to be aware of in 2017, look no further!"

NATALIE SISSSON
The "Suitcase Entrepreneur"
@nataliesisson

"David's ability to identify and engage so many leading minds in the industry is a testament to both his standing in the community and awareness of how real-world digital marketing problems need to be tackled. Community has always been key to the advancement of this field that is constantly challenged by the flux of human behaviours, technological advancements and algorithms. Each marketer in 'Digital Marketing in 2017' has a different window and set of data, collating observations en masse allows for the reader to see both the factors that are currently presenting as consistent, but also illustrates those that are emerging. Highly recommended!"

LEXI MILLS
SEO PR Expert
@leximills

TO MUM, DAD & ADELINE

CONTENTS

ACKNOWLEDGMENTS

A very special thanks to Jonny Ross from *jrc.agency* and Alex Tachalova from *DigitalOlympus.net*. As publishing partners to *'Digital Marketing in 2017'* you have both made a massive difference in helping to make this dream become a reality.

***

A big thanks to the 107 digital marketing experts who contributed so generously to this project. Each and every one of you has provided such significant value. The digital marketing community is a really special place. Long may it continue!

***

FOREWORD BY MARK ASQUITH

Digital Marketing. A phrase that used to singlehandedly scare the wits out of even the savviest print marketer and make small businesses fear the very idea of needing to change what had always worked for them.

We were sold SEO, single-page "landing sites" and backlinks galore, all in the pursuit of "conquering digital marketing", by marketers who had no more an idea of what digital marketing meant for them or their customers than I do of the difference between a driveshaft and a piston.

But, time is the great leveller, and as time progressed we were all able to look at this developing landscape and judge for ourselves what worked and what didn't work for our businesses.

And here we stand today: digital marketing in 2017 is now simply "marketing".

The role that digital plays in any business is undeniable and as that role grows, so does the plethora of disciplines, techniques and metrics within this once "catch-all" area of your company.

The reality of digital marketing in 2017 is that there is so much information available to each and every one of us – with advances happening every single day – that overwhelm can set in and force digital marketing into being a "check box" in a meeting that saps up valuable time and budget but doesn't return anything of genuine value to you, or your business.

Perhaps we can no longer call ourselves "digital marketers".

As marketers, we live in the age of specialism and as a specialist in one or two disciplines, we find ourselves struggling to keep momentum with the other disciplines that exist in digital marketing.

In fact, our single biggest challenge is navigating the ever-changing path that lies before us digitally.

Every single one of us needs a trusted guide.

Every single one of us needs someone to whom we can look to for wisdom, guidance and connection to the wider realm of digital marketing and someone who is willing to give us honest, tested and most of all trusted feedback on the digital marketing world as it stands on any given day.

In 2014 I launched my first "real" podcast.

Despite being a marketer for almost ten years at that point,

I was scared and felt vulnerable letting my voice run wild in front of strangers who I genuinely believed would judge me, a "Northern monkey" from Barnsley "preaching" about business and marketing.

And, at that point, my skills as a digital marketer needed a little polish, to say the least.

I'd focused so hard on building my design agency that I'd forgotten the subtle art of keeping my knowledge at the cutting edge of the industry and, being completely frank, I felt out of my depth.

And then I met my own trusted guide, David Bain.

Being invited to guest on David's flagship show, "*Digital Marketing Radio*" was a milestone in the path to where I am today. Because on that show, I found my guide.

David's quiet confidence, proven business acumen and heritage in what was a nascent industry when he built his first digital product, a restaurant booking platform, endeared me to him immediately and we instantly struck up a bond that began with me ribbing David about his wild technical set up and crazy green screen antics; my beard receiving the same kind of "feedback" every time we speak.

David's friendship and guidance is something I *know* that I can rely upon. And observing how David has created this mammoth, entirely value-driven book that enables you and me to elevate ourselves, simply reinforces my belief that there is no one more qualified in the UK, heck the world, to be **your** trusted guide in this ever-growing and sometimes daunting world of digital marketing.

"Aw that's lovely, but what about the book?"

This book, simply put, is full of the most proven and tested digital marketing advice in the world.

Through his drive and desire to pull together the very best advice, David has drawn upon such a high-quality, successful network of digital marketers that the opportunity to simply *read* this book, never mind *action* some of its teachings, is a chance that you simply cannot miss.

This book is your blueprint to digital marketing confidence.

If David is the trusted guide, then this book is the map by which he guides us all to achieving the goals that we set ourselves online.

You see, we live in the world of the platform.

Snapchat, Instagram, Facebook, Twitter, Periscope. I could go on almost indefinitely digging into the platforms that exist to give us an opportunity to market to our prospects and customers.

Too eager are we to "dive in" to creating, to "marketing" and to simply "using" these platforms that we forget not only *why* we're doing it, but we forget to spend the time looking at *how* we can do it *properly* and *optimally*.

Digital Marketing in 2017 breaks down every major, functional facet of digital marketing as it stands today and gives you a clear overview, action set and call to action to make **that** part of digital marketing work at the very highest level for you.

Individually, the tactics in this book are a powerful set of tools that you can add to your business gradually and successfully.

Strung together, the teachings in this book will transform **you** from a competent user of digital marketing technologies to a confident and proven strategic thinker and patient, conscientious and results-driven marketer for life.

The beauty of what David has so elegantly put together with this book is that no matter your current experience, you will find new ways to generate results and be inspired to experiment with processes, tools and strategies that you believe to be reserved for the "big guys".

ALL business, from small business to big business, can learn to overcome digital marketing fear, procrastination and waste with the use of this book and don't worry, your time will be maximised thanks to the flow of the book that David has crafted.

Start from the beginning or simply dive in; pick a specialism or choose to learn more about them all, the choice is yours.

"Digital Marketing". A phrase that, in 2017, will inspire, elevate and reward you.

Mark Asquith
January 2017

DAVID BAIN

BACKGROUND

Ten years ago, in early 2007, I presented my first digital marketing seminar. I called it the '*13 Pillars of Internet Marketing*'. In fact, you can still view it on YouTube.

Back then, digital marketing – or 'internet marketing' as it was more commonly called, was small enough to be a single topic. I never heard of anyone specialising in just a section of digital marketing. That seemed too niche back then.

The '*13 Pillars of Internet Marketing*' morphed into the '*26-Week Digital Marketing Plan*' and it was that that I honed and delivered as an in-person seminar across the UK over the next couple of years.

Over the years after that, I continued to update my *26-Week Digital Marketing Plan* – up until 2014. The online version that I poured my heart and soul into in early 2014 includes more than 26 hours of video training. Just me, sharing as much as I could over 26 hours of video.

I knew as I was finishing up that version of the 26-Week Plan that it wouldn't be sane for me to try to do it again, at least just by myself without any help. So I took a little break while I decided what I wanted to do next.

By the summer of 2014 I knew what I should do. I'd always loved podcasting – I'd dabbled in it since 2006. "That's what I'll do" I thought to myself. I'll start a podcast that interviews all the top digital marketers on their specific area of expertise.

At the same time, I wanted to produce a highly professional sounding show. I knew that when I listed to podcasts myself, I switched off when the audio quality was poor.

After a LOT of research I ordered what I considered to be the best equipment (An *RE-20* microphone, a *Soundcraft* mixer and a *Zoom H5* audio recorder if you're interested) and set about mastering how to produce the best quality sound.

In August 2014 *Digital Marketing Radio* was born. And since then I've had the pleasure and privilege of interviewing over 180 niche digital marketing experts on their specialist subject.

I didn't know precisely what I was going to get out of it. All I knew was that I wanted to do it, and that if I stuck with it, and did a great job, I'd gain so much. Many things that I hadn't even considered.

And that's exactly what happened. Every single week – if

not more often – I interviewed a top digital marketing expert. I was consistent – some shows attracted more listeners than others, but that wasn't a concern. I just wanted to make them as good as possible, and be consistent.

By November 2015 I'd interviewed around 120 experts. I'd started to live broadcast each interview and it seemed like the time was right to arrange the next challenge. I wanted to invite everyone who had been on the show so far to all be on a live, one-off digital marketing predictions show.

Thankfully, 54 of the experts that I'd already interviewed were able to make it for the December 2015 live special – you can watch a replay of that show here: *DigitalMarketingRadio.com/2016predictions*.

It went really well. Virtually every guest was able to join me bang-on schedule. And thanks to the technology (*Blab* – which unfortunately no longer exists), I was able to manage the appearances of all my guests on single 2-hour show.

Fast forward to November 2016 and I was ready to do it again. By this stage I'd interviewed 180 guests and I was ready to do something even bigger. (I don't like making life easy on myself!)

So for the December 2016 show I wanted to have over 100 live guests. However, unfortunately as I mentioned above, *Blab* no longer existed by this stage. This meant that I had to find some other solution to make this whole thing work!

N.B. The only change that I wanted to make for the

December 2016 show was to turn it into a digital marketing tip, rather than a prediction that the guests shared. I wanted to make it as actionable as possible for the viewers.

I'd already been broadcasting regular *Digital Marketing Radio* shows the previous couple of months, live on *Facebook* – and I decided that broadcasting the whole show on *Facebook Live* would probably bring me strong audience figures.

The challenge was how to bring all the guests in. *Facebook Live* didn't have any native functionality to bring in guests – and certainly not over a hundred of them on the same show.

So what I did was to ask all of my guests to join me in a private *Google Hangout*. I then took that video and audio and combined it with my own video and audio, and used specialist online streaming software (*vMix*) to broadcast the combined video live on *Facebook*.

Unfortunately there were a few challenges! Everything appeared to be going swimmingly from my end to begin with, however, taking the opportunity to read a few comments from some of the live *Facebook* viewers; it quickly became apparent that not everything was as it should have been.

Apparently those watching live could see and hear me fine. They could see my guests fine too, but not hear them. Not what I needed!

It meant that I had to figure-out the audio issues and resolve them – plus host a 4-hour video show – all at the same time!

Thankfully I had some help from the fantastic Olga Andrienko from *SEMRush* over the first 45 minutes or so. Olga jumped in as temporary host while I tried to resolve my technical issues.

I eventually fixed the sound gremlins, but I did have a few more technical challenges over the course of the show meaning that I ended up rebooting the *Facebook Live* stream 3 or 4 times.

This meant that my dreams of having thousands of people watch live didn't happen – and it also meant that I wasn't willing to pay to boost the original show recordings on Facebook (bearing in mind the technical challenges that were plain to see).

I could have got down about this, but the facts are – as Jeff Sauer said during the show – I don't think anyone else has done this before. I'm doing something unique by bringing over 100 guests onto the same show, giving each guest just 2 minutes to share their top piece of wisdom.

No. I should be proud that I'm pushing the boundaries so hard that issues happen along the way. After all, as the old saying goes – it's not how far you fall, but how high you bounce that counts.

One thing I learned in my early podcasting days was that you need to be recording your audio and video content in multiple places.

And thank goodness that's what I did. My audio and my

guests' audio was also being recorded in my trusty *Zoom H5*. And my guests' video was also being recorded on *YouTube*.

Although it would be a pain, this meant that I could edit the recordings afterwards to create a much smoother viewing experience. And this, dear reader is what I'm going to do just after I finish this book.

This book – *Digital Marketing in 2017* – is a categorised written reproduction of every single tip shared on that December 2016 show.

But – and I hope you agree – it's much better than a transcript. To begin with, I didn't know what my guests were going to share, and it what order. This book means that I've had an opportunity to re-order the guest sequence based upon how each tip fits together.

Secondly, I've edited each tip a touch. Not to change the advice given, but to try to ensure that everything reads as well as it can, and to draw a thread through the wonderful advice. I have left in occasional references to the live show, where it made sense to leave them in.

As I mentioned, as soon as this book is published, it is my intention to publish those edited set of video recordings on *DigitalMarketingRadio.com*. Those should be published in February and March 2017. If you're reading this after that period, you should be able to check those recordings out on the website.

The additional good news for you though dear reader is that I've arranged a very special set of bonuses for you – just for reading this book! So if you haven't done so already, make sure that you sign up for your exclusive bonuses at *DigitalMarketingRadio.com/book*.

Finally, if you haven't checked out *jrc.agency* and *DigitalOlympus.net* please do so. Jonny Ross, founder of *jrc.agency* has been a long-term supporter of *Digital Marketing Radio* and he kindly agreed to be one of the publishing partners of this very book. Jonny and his team – special mention to Helen Robinson – have been integral in the production of the content for this book. Check out Jonny's award-winning digital marketing blog over at *jrc.agency*.

And special thanks to Alex Tachalova, founder of *DigitalOlympus.net*. Alex provided a few of the guests for the show with her wonderful contacts and she also helped a great deal with the promotion of the event. *Digital Olympus* is a quarterly free event with live training sessions from some of the world's leading digital experts. If you haven't signed up for Alex's next event, I highly recommend that you do so now over at *DigitalOlympus.net*.

Now, on with the show…

David Bain
January 2017

1 GET STARTED

So many digital marketing possibilities. Where to begin?

The temptation is often to start afresh. To light the touchpaper on a fresh project, marking the start of a new year. But that's not what Tim Matthews, author of '*The Professional Marketer*' is doing.

1) Integration is key – Tim Matthews

Tim says: "The biggest challenge I see in 2017 and beyond is integration. And what I mean by that is we have so many new marketing technologies, and there's so much bad data still in the system.

"For 2017, my goal is to clean up my act. Clean up my data, and understand where my leads are coming from, and where my influence is coming from."

Lesson one – it's likely that gold will be found in your existing analytics... but only if you have good data. Clean up your own data and vow to maintain good data from now on.

> *"Gold is to be found in your own analytics...*
> *but only if you have good data."*
> **TIM MATTHEWS**
> *@timmatthewssv*

But apart from ensuring the health of our recordkeeping, are there any issues with the way that we're currently working?

2) Break down your silos – Stewart Rogers

Stewart Rogers, journalist, analyst, and speaker from the daily tech news publication *Venture Beat* believes that marketers need to stop treating opportunities as silos.

Stewart says: "I want to talk to you very briefly about mobile in terms of what the opportunity is. Mobile this year in the United States alone is going to (in effect) influence 500 billion dollars' worth of sales in the very latest numbers, in terms of sales that are actually happening on mobile devices.

"In terms of m-commerce there is a 140-billion-dollar opportunity. 70% of people are now doing research on mobile before doing a store visit. So, the smartphone is relevant and incredibly important.

"Will they spend more money is 2017 than 2016? Yes. In fact, only 12% of consumers will spend less in 2017 than they did in 2016, so mobile is the number one thing.

"There's a problem though – and this is a thing we need to fix… and this is my tip for 2017.

"It turns out, regardless of whether you have 55,000 dollars or pounds in your marketing budget, or you've got 50 million, the issues are the same. You are putting a huge amount of prevalence and importance on mobile.

"In fact many of you, a third of you, are spending 50% of your budget on mobile, but you all agree – mostly – that you don't know what you're doing!

"It's just tacked on the end of your existing channels. There's not a strategy. Partly that is a technology issue but mostly it's a silo issue.

"Many of you, a third of you, are spending 50% of your budget on mobile, but you all agree, mostly, that you don't know what you're doing."
STEWART ROGERS
@TheRealSJR

"My top tip for 2017 is please break down these silos rather than just adding mobile as a tac on the end of a channel, because that is what is breaking everything.

"Be mindful of what is happening over the next 20 days. Don't worry about the future in 20 years, just worry about the future over the next 20 days.

"Think about artificial intelligence for 2017, with chat bots as part of that story. Virtual reality is massive. Make sure you're understanding that and leveraging that. It's where you can do some amazing things from the point of view of extremely unique content, which is the only way to get noticed now."

Stewart highlights many of the areas that will be touched upon in greater depth later on in this book.

However, his main point follows on from Tim Matthew's initial thoughts – that integration will be key in 2017. And that unless you understand the context between various customer touch points and the context between different forms of marketing, you won't be optimising your activities.

3) Where to start? Do your dishes – Yaro Starak

However, it's sometimes difficult to know where to start, and this is where Yaro Starak's thoughts come in useful. Yaro is Founder of the popular blog *Entrepreneur's Journey*.

I first interviewed Yaro way back in 2007 and he always seems to have an original perspective on things.

When asked to provide a digital marketing tip for 2017, Yaro said: "I thought about this and I had all of the typical answers that many people say, such as search engine optimisation, social media marketing, doing joint ventures, affiliate marketing and buying ads.

"I really thought back to what's worked for me and I think will continue to work, and this is going to sound really crazy but my big marketing tip for you is to do your dishes.

"Now let me explain what I mean by that. In my experience, one of the biggest blockages to getting that traffic and building your business is a lack of momentum.

"Momentum for me really comes from starting with something small – and when I say small, it doesn't even have to be business. It can be something like waking up, having a shower, brushing your teeth, and then going to do your dishes.

"Momentum for me really comes from starting with something small and when I say small, it doesn't even have to be business."
YARO STARAK
@yarostarak

"If someone is taking some action towards the start of a day, it actually starts to build momentum. I find the energy then carries through to doing the marketing activities, or any other activities within your business.

"I personally don't think people are lacking ideas when it comes to marketing. It's actually taking the initial steps that's important. What gives you the energy, what gives you the action, what makes you productive.

"For me – if I'm ever feeling lazy, if I don't want to do the work or I'm procrastinating, just doing something really simple like cleaning the dishes, taking out the trash, fixing something you meant to fix around the house is the kick-start you need to then go and do what marketing activities you have on your list. 'Do the dishes' is my advice."

What initially sounded almost like a flippant response is actually quite enlightening. The key is to try not to procrastinate. Keep moving and you'll slowly head in the right direction. Just start somewhere.

Chapter 1: Get Started – summary

- Start by cleaning up your existing data
- Commit to maintaining your new data in an orderly manner
- Understand where your leads are coming from
- Know that mobile is key, but don't treat it as a silo
- Don't get overwhelmed, just do something – anything to get started

2 DESIGN & STRUCTURE

Some readers of *Digital Marketing in 2017* will be quite technical in their understanding of areas such as SEO, coding and website design. Others may be more creative and have less of a 'technical brain'.

Whatever your degree of familiarity may be with coding and the like, the fact of the matter is that great digital performance – in part – relies on a heathy site structure. And the next couple of chapters focus on helping you to achieve that.

So if you don't have too many scientific bones in your body, bear with me. But also try to stick with it, in the knowledge that a lot of digital marketers view these areas as being essential to success in 2017 and beyond. Don't ignore something just because it doesn't capture your imagination as much.

4) Use eye tracking and split-testing before the build stage – Joshua Strawczynski

Joshua Strawczynski from *J Marketing* emphasises the importance of thinking about optimising conversion rates before a site design is finalised.

Josh says: "We're really focusing on advertising effectiveness – and we're doing this having invested heavily in eye tracking software.

"Whether it is landing pages, banner design or even the effectiveness of content, we are running it through eye tracking, which has traditionally been very expensive. We've been able to make that and A/B testing very affordable.

"Before it ever goes to the build stage, [your user experience] has to be absolutely bang on."

> *"Before it ever goes to the build stage, [your user experience] has to be absolutely bang on."*
> **JOSH STRAWCZYNSKI**
> *@JoshStraw84*

[Editor's note: Hotjar is one of the world's leading heatmapping and user feedback software platforms. And Hotjar's founder – Dr David Darmanin – has kindly offered two month's free access to Hotjar's business plan (worth 178 euros) to all 'Digital Marketing in 2017' readers. Register for this and other bonuses at DigitalMarketingRadio.com/book.]

5) Focus on speed – Michael Stricker

Part of great user experience is ensuring that your site loads as fast as possible. That's the tip that *MS Design*'s Lead Consultant, Michael Stricker shares.

Michael says: "As I've only got two minutes to share my tip, I thought of speed.

"I was just on *Digital Olympus*, talking about 'four things you can do to encourage a conversion with your visitors'. And if you can't get people to move quickly across your site, or a crawler [bot] to move quickly across your site, you're sunk.

> *"If you can't get people to move quickly across your site, or a crawler [bot] to move quickly across your site, you're sunk."*
> **MICHAEL STRICKER**
> *@RadioMS*

"Right now, mobile is two out of every three minutes that Americans spend on digital media. That's from *comScore*. So, knowing that puts America finally in the same place as much of the rest of the world.

"I read a post today called 'Should you be focusing on a mobile-first campaign strategy', and my thought to that was 'Yes!' You absolutely must focus. And you need to analyse. You need to focus on the competition. You need to think about comparing yourself to others.

"There's just so much focus on mobile – and if you're not

working on speeding-up your site, you will lose."

6) Think mobile first – Dan Taylor

Focusing on mobile is also a message that resonates with Dan Taylor, Technical SEO Consultant and Account Manager at *Salt Agency*.

Dan says: "Two things that I feel go hand-in-hand in 2017 are growth of mobile search and voice search.

> *"Focus on going mobile first with your website, disregarding building desktop to begin with."*
> **DAN TAYLOR**
> *@danny_taywitter*

He continues: "In 2016 it's been pretty obvious that globally, search engines have been moving towards mobile.

"It started off with the Vladivostok update from *Yandex* and then the second *Google* update at the start of the year, accelerated mobile pages (AMP) becoming mainstream – and even to an certain extent *Baidu*'s mobile site builder. It's important to classify that voice search goes with that too.

"I've seen noticeably on commutes that more people are using the voice search feature – and I feel that one of the biggest things from that is going to be optimising content for voice search, as opposed to just general keywords.

"The way we speak is in a much more semantic nature [than typing]. We obviously speak long-form as opposed to saying just two or three keywords.

"My top tip for 2017 would be to focus on going mobile-first with your website, disregarding building desktop to begin with.

"Desktop should be the afterthought. Getting your structured data and your semantic markup in-place within your content should be the next step."

7) It's the year of mobile, again – Ryan Buchanan

As Ryan Buchanan from *eROI* says, people have been claiming that it's the year of mobile for a while now. But it really is the year of mobile now.

Ryan says: "I think the big stat that stood out for me for cyber Monday is in one day, mobile e-commerce went over a billion dollars – just in one day. That's 35% up from last year. So my tip is streamlining and simplifying the mobile purchase process.

> *"My tip is streamlining and simplifying the mobile purchase process."*
> **RYAN BUCHANAN**
> *@ryanbuch*

"The action is to look at your site and try to remove any barriers along the mobile website or checkout process. We've been saying it's the year of mobile for the last fifteen years – but it's really real now."

8) Use progressive web apps – Tony Passey

Tony Passey, Digital Marketing Professor at *University of Utah* & CEO/Founder at *FireToss* is doing everything in his power to ensure that his designers always think mobile-first.

Tony says: "We're forcing our designers to stop designing for desktop – we're literally taking the desktop option away from them. And we're getting all websites to be designed on the mobile device first and foremost.

"So many people think about the building of their website in terms of a desktop, and then a tablet. And then mobile is the third thought – we can't do that anymore.

"As you look at so many wonderful applications on the web, mobile is an afterthought. In order to support that technology and that shift in paradigm, marketers should look at Google's AMP project as a better way to serve mobile pages, because there is a real genuine speed increase.

> *"If you're just now arriving to AMP then stop, skip it and move on to progressive web apps."*
> **TONY PASSEY**
> *@tonypassey*

"I think that all of us that observe search traffic see that AMP pages are loading faster and ranking much higher on search engines.

"I feel like if you don't know what AMP is, you're way behind the times. If you're just now arriving at AMP then stop, skip it and move on to PWAs. Learn what PWAs are, how to build them, and force your developers or yourself to learn how to develop all your web technologies that are built for mobile in PWAs.

"If you don't know what that is, it's basically the ability for you to handle functions on a mobile website similar to how you can handle them within an in-app experience.

"If you don't know where to begin there, a really good place to begin is to look at *firebase.google.com* – *Google*'s sponsored firebase project. It's an entire base of code, explanations, learning tools, and all kinds of resources to teach you how to build PWAs.

"We've all seen this in the last three or four years. Mobile has just taken over the planet and I don't feel like it's stopping.

"I feel there will always be a small niche for desktop and tablet but I think mobile continues to get richer and the experience gets better, and if you haven't changed your development and design process, as of now, you're losing."

9) Organise your digital team structure – Jonnie Jensen

The last element of this chapter, 'design & structure' isn't about the design of your web presence. It's about the design and structure of your own digital team – and that's something that Jonnie Jenson, Founder of *Live and Social* is passionate about.

Jonnie says: "I want to recommend and encourage people

to look at the structure of their team. Digital leadership is so, so important.

"People look at why their digital strategy, social media and content is failing and why they can't get the support from their company. Ultimately it comes down to the leadership and the structure of their teams.

"What I want people to realise is that they need a strong digital leader, someone who understands everything from the website design to SEO, to PPC, to online advertising.

"The structure of the team beneath them in a big company should be one person per role. And in a small company these roles might just need to be different hats you need to wear.

> *"Start from the top, have leaders who understand digital – then recruit properly and resource appropriately for the size of your business."*
> **JONNIE JENSEN**
> *@JonnieJensen*

"You need to have someone whose accountability it is to be a content and community manager – someone who is looking after the community, creating content, engaging with people, looking to grow the reach.

"You need a campaign manager, looking at how they can generate business through acquisition, online advertising, re-targeting through social ads, the automation behind it, the work-flows, the emails.

"The campaign manager is really a numbers-focused person and community managers aren't often good at the numbers. The numbers people often aren't good at the communication. So they are very different roles.

"The third role is the customer service role, looking after reputation, looking after Net Promoter Score, making sure if complaints are coming in that they are dealt with in an appropriate and prompt manner.

"These roles are the hallmarks of a successful, digital strategy. And ultimately what creates market leaders.

"Many business leaders don't have the knowledge and skills, yet they end up trying to run or try to hire a team of digital people – and then they just fall flat on their face.

"Start from the top, have leaders who understand digital – then recruit properly and resource appropriately for the size of your business."

[Editor's note: Jonnie had generously shared a full copy of his digital marketing team structure with the readers of this book. Register at DigitalMarketingRadio.com/book to obtain this, and the rest of the bonus materials.]

Chapter 2: Design & Structure – summary

- Test your user experience before you even get to the website build stage
- Make sure your website loads as quickly as possible – for bots as well as users
- Focus on going mobile-first with your website, disregarding building desktop to begin with
- Remove any barriers in your mobile site customer journey
- If you're just arriving at AMP then stop, skip it and move on to progressive web apps (PWAs)
- Design a structure for your digital team – then recruit to fill the structure

3 TECHNICAL SEO

This is the second of the two chapters that deal with the more technical aspects of digital marketing in 2017. Get through this one and you're over the hump!

An essential part of technical SEO ensures that your website includes markup code that helps search engines to understand your content better.

10) Featured snippets – AJ Ghergich

It's possible to encourage *Google* to include some of your content in their search results – featured snippets. This is something that AJ Ghergich, SEO & Content Marketing Expert at *Ghergich.com* is currently incorporating into his client services.

AJ says: "We're focusing our clients on earning featured

snippets – mainly because it's a new part of an effective content marketing strategy.

"We've recently done a study with *SEMRush* (I have it pinned on my twitter handle *@SEO*) with a lot of useful takeaways for feature snippets. You can go in there and see exactly how you should format your content to fit each specific snippet that you're going after."

"We're focusing our clients on earning featured snippets [in 2017]."
AJ GHERGICH
@SEO

11) Get great with structured data – Bridget Randolph

Someone else currently working on getting *Google* to understand and feature more of her client's content is Bridget Randolph from *BridgetRandolph.com.*

Bridget says: "The thing that I'm telling everyone at the moment is to think about how to make your content specific to your website, but also how to make it for things like apps.

"We've already talked about whether content was mobile friendly, but that still limits you to mobile screens. Whereas, with structured data we're more able than ever to send content and display it in the way that is most suitable to the format that that the device or location suits.

"The practical application of this for this coming year is

getting good with structured data. Understanding what *Google*'s doing with things like Rich Cards. Think ahead a little bit.

"Start asking yourself things like 'would a personal assistant app understand what my content is about?' 'Would a smart watch make sense of this? Or a TV?'. Think about how different devices might display your content."

> *"Start asking yourself things like 'would a personal assistant app understand what my content is about?"*
>
> **BRIDGET RANDOLPH**
> *@BridgetRandolph*

12) Page speed, structured data & machine learning – Mike King

Mike King, Founder of *iPullRank* delivers another vote for harnessing the power of structured data.

Mike says: "My tip for 2017 is largely about page speed, structured data and machine learning.

"Essentially what I am saying is that if you follow the things that *Google* is doing from a development perspective, you're going to continue being ahead. And these are the things that they have been focusing on so much over the last year or so, and will continue to do so.

"Looking at progressive web apps, looking at AMP, you can tell their progression is very much about speed. And when you think about these new applications like voice search, *Google Home*, and all these other things, they're all about making that 'Star Trek computer'. What really supports that is going to be site speed, and also structured data.

"Get ahead and build the right sort of structured data on your site, and then think about what you can do to leverage machine learning. Because there are so many great marketing applications that are going to help out there.

> *"If you follow the things that Google is doing from a development perspective, you're going to continue being ahead."*
> **MIKE KING**
> **@iPullRank**

But if we're talking about search, there is a lot of untapped potential and I think that there's a lot of opportunity for marketers to get ahead right now with some of the existing tools."

So keep an eye on the future, but take advantage of the technology that's available to you now to be different – and because of that, better than the competition.

13) Take advantage of HTTP/2 – Mark Thomas

One technology that not all of your competitors will be utilising at the moment is HTTP/2. And Mark Thomas, VP of Growth at *Botify* says that this is definitely a technology that you should embrace.

Mark says: "My big tip is to ensure people are adopting

HTTP/2. The speed gains of using the new protocol could be up to 15% quicker load times – just because you're using HTTP/2.

"To take advantage of that, the actionable thing you need to do is make sure you've migrated to HTTPS. Because Chrome and Firefox only support the protocol by default on an encrypted line.

"I still think there's a staggering number of sites ranging from the *BBC* to *Bloomingdales* that haven't migrated.

"There's a big opportunity there for everyone that is migrating to HTTP/2, which stands at about 11% of the internet as things stand.

> *"Make sure you're employing and adopting HTTP/2."*
> **MARK THOMAS**
> *@SearchMATH*

"*WordPress* and *Cloudflare* have already moved, so people using them will already have the opportunity. But it's one that I think everyone should take, because there are some much bigger things coming along. I think getting this migration done in 2017 is important.

"You've heard a lot about AMP. You might skip AMP, and move to PWA as some people have already been saying.

It's a really exciting time with new technologies that can run with new protocols, such as HTTP/2. So my actionable tip is to make sure you're employing and adopting HTTP/2."

14) Keep a close eye on AMP – **Barry Adams**

Mark Tomas above and Tony Passey in the previous chapter both talked about the possibility of bypassing AMP, and AMP certainly seems like a hot topic at the moment. Barry Adams, Founder of *Polemic Digital* also believes it's important.

Barry says: "I want to talk about *Google*'s Accelerated Mobile Pages, and why I think it's going to be very important. I'm a bit ambivalent about it if I'm entirely honest because I'm not a big fan of *Google* forcing another web standard down our throats.

> *"Keep a very close eye on what AMP is doing and to be prepared to switch tactics."*
> **BARRY ADAMS**
> *@badams*

"But I can see what they are trying to do. And the most powerful aspect about it is something I don't think the majority of people necessarily understand, which is that *Google* will preload AMP results on its own *Google* cache, and then preload them in mobile web browsers, which is exactly what's providing that very fast experience on AMP pages.

"There's a lot of activity on the roadmap to develop AMP further with all kinds of new features and functionality being introduced, such as getting AMP working for e-commerce scenarios.

"I expect 2017 to be the year that will prove AMP to be a very dominant force going forward, or it might turn out to be a bit of a dud and people will abandon it because there's just not enough mass behind it as we've seen with Google's experiments over the years.

"My advice would be to keep a very close eye on what AMP is doing and to be prepared to switch tactics – and adopting AMP very quickly as the need arises."

15) Another vote for AMP pages – Jonny Ross

Someone who's quite certain about the value of AMP now is Jonny Ross, MD and Founder of *Jonny Ross Consultancy*.

Jonny says: "It's ultimately a really lightweight, stripped down version of your web page.

"*Google* has announced that 40% of people abandon a web page if it takes more than three seconds to load. I'm not sure how true that is, but I know we all expect things instantly. And the average load speed for an AMP page is 0.7 seconds.

"By having AMP pages, you can rank very high in *Google*. You get featured at the top of *Google*. The latest stats show that the top position of *Google* gets 31% of the click-through rate, position two gets 19%.

"So you're looking at 50% of the clicks in just the top two positions of *Google* search results. By creating an AMP page, you've got a very good chance of being in that top position in *Google*.

"By creating an AMP page, you've got a very good chance of being in that top position in Google."

JONNY ROSS
@jonnyross

"There's downsides, there are some negatives. Duplication is one of the biggest ones, so it's important to use canonical tags correctly.

"However, the whole thing comes back to content. There's no point having AMP pages unless you have amazing content.

"So from that perspective, nothing has changed for 2017: it's about fabulous, great content that's very focused, that's very 'target-audienced'.

"Think of personas, who are you writing for, what's the purpose of writing, and write with the target audience in mind. As long as you create good content, you're onto a winner in 2017."

16) AMP, progressive web apps & voice search – Gianluca Fiorelli

Voicing his opinion on AMP, progressive web apps and voice search is Gianluca Fiorelli from *iLoveSEO.net*.

Gianluca says: "I have started putting together a timeline of what *Google* tells us during the year, and at the same time also including a note of the companies that they buy during that period.

"From this timeline, what I can tell you is two substantial things about the next year. Firstly, if you go to *Google*'s blog, 90% of the posts have been about mobile since March 2016. Many of them are about AMP.

"From this, we can stress the importance of including AMP as part of your strategy. And not only for news. We also now see AMP used by several e-commerce websites. Which means moving forward, you should start thinking about progressive web applications (PWAs). Over the last couple of months *Google* has started to express a lot of love for PWAs.

> *"Talking about voice search, don't forget about Bing. Because Bing powers the voice searches of Alexa, Siri and obviously Cortana."*
> **GIANLUCA FIORELLI**
> **@ *gfiorelli1***

"Secondly, voice search. All the patents that *Google* is publishing at the moment are related to natural language. And that means voice search.

"Talking about voice search, don't forget about *Bing*. Because *Bing* powers the voice searches of *Alexa*, *Siri* and obviously *Cortana*. We always talk about *Google*, but perhaps *Bing* will grab a larger piece of the search market through voice search. Those would be my two things to think about for 2017."

17) Everything affects everything – Dawn Anderson

Concluding chapter three, Dawn Anderson from *Move It Marketing* talks about how SEOs need to be juggling multiple balls.

Dawn says: "Whilst this is not necessarily within the remit of the SEO practitioner, everything affects everything, and optimising the experience cross-device should be seen as high priority.

"Everything affects everything and optimising the experience cross-device should be seen as high priority."
DAWN ANDERSON
@dawnieando

"We all know that the search engines are focusing a lot of effort on machine learning, and this has been a huge fascination in the SEO community in 2016; however there is still plenty of work to do in 'business as usual'.

"It's often very easy to go chasing the 'shiny things' all the time, yet there are good old fashioned text-book SEO areas left neglected. These include fixing many of the technical SEO issues which abound, and revisiting tired content.

"Optimising existing content for readability and re-purposing or 'enriching' to adapt to the rise of 'voice search' and featured snippets via answering questions is low-hanging-fruit that should not be ignored.

"Also add videos and multiple sections to up-cycle evergreen content that still meets needs, but just needs some polish applying.

"And of course: ... go AMP and HTTPS."

Chapter 3: Technical SEO – summary

- Give your website a better chance of being included in *Google*'s 'featured snippets'
- Test what your content looks like on TVs, smart watches and other platforms
- Follow the things that *Google* is doing from a development perspective and you'll stay ahead
- Make sure you're employing and adopting HTTP/2
- Keep a very close eye on what AMP is doing and be prepared to switch tactics
- There's no point in having AMP pages unless you have amazing content
- Don't forget about *Bing*. *Bing* powers the voice searches of *Alexa*, *Siri* and *Cortana*
- Optimising the cross-device experience should be seen as priority

DAVID BAIN

4 CUSTOMER JOURNEYS

Now it's time to move on from making your website perform as effectively as possible from a technical perspective, to really starting to understand your target clientele and how they interact with your 'funnel'.

18) Focus on the buyer's journey – Olga Andrienko

For Olga Andrienko, Head of Social at *SEMRush*, it's all about defining precisely who your ideal client is.

Olga says: "My top tip would be to think through the buyer's journey more. I see that some companies really pay attention to it. Some don't.

"It's the consumer that now really defines the way we communicate with them, and also how we reach out to them.

"The time for viral campaigns is over. Now's the time for personalised campaigns. And that's why we're into split-testing.

"I suggest that companies define their target audience as one ideal client. And then work through the buyer journey with that client."
OLGA ANDRIENKO
@Olgandrienko

"I suggest that companies define their target audience as one ideal client. And then work through the buyer journey with that client, encouraging them to go from brand awareness to brand advocacy.

"The most important thing is that the target audience finds the right content as part of the buyers' journey.

"I also see a trend moving towards closed communities with smaller audiences and higher attention spans. Because attention is today's digital currency.

"Companies should tap into the closed communities and content marketing opportunities on *Facebook*. For instance, *Facebook* blogs would be a good thing for international and global companies to do. Because these companies are 24/7. And it would help their clients to easily reach out to [the businesses] whenever they wish. That would be an amazing thing to do in 2017."

19) Double-down on understanding your buyers – Art Jones

Understanding your buyers better is also a subject that resonates with Art Jones, Founder of *ArtJones.tv*.

Art says: "I believe there is one prediction that always rules them all. In 2017, like every other year, the intention of marketing is to call an audience to take action (to buy my stuff!). I submit therefore that understanding the buyer's persona and buyer's journeys should be the number one job for 2017.

"In 2017 I am doubling down on understanding my ideal buyers' narrative, with the intention to know them almost as well as they know themselves.

"When we begin each marketing campaign with the intention to do the work to understand our ideal buyer, we position ourselves to create great content and great experiences in the proper context – to reach, engage and nurture conversations.

> *"Begin 2017 by taking a healthy dose of empathy and get to know your ideal buyers."*
> **ART JONES**
> **@ ArtJones**

"Our buyers are not a field in a column on a spreadsheet. Our buyers are real people that celebrate their wins and agonise over the challenges they face, just like we do.

"Begin 2017 by taking a healthy dose of empathy and get to know your ideal buyers."

20) Focus on creating great customer experiences – Alita Harvey-Rodriguez

But it's not just about understanding your buyer. As Alita Harvey-Rodriguez, Founder of *Milk IT Academy* says, you need to focus on creating great customer experiences.

Alita says: "Something that's become very apparent this year is customer-first content. And the need to drive our content from a place that has nothing to do with our products, but more about *the why*. Not your why, but the why of the customers. And the need to deeply understand the customer journey."

> *"Push marketing is just not going to cut it any more. We need to be personalising, nurturing and investing in customer-first content."*
> **ALITA HARVEY-RODRIGUEZ**
> *@MsAlitaHR*

"People really expect experience now. They're not just purchasing from a company because it's their local company. They're not just purchasing from a company because it's their only choice. People have choice. And they need to have a great experience when they go and purchase from a brand.

"That comes from everything from retail, right into hospitality. You're not going to walk in somewhere, you're not going to talk about something if you haven't got the experience that you want.

"People talk about experience. They don't talk about anything else. If we've had a positive one then we're going to talk about it a lot more. One-to-one communications isn't a 'nice to have', it's a 'need to have' now.

"We really need to be investing in marketing automation, and drip-feeding our content based on where that customer is at that particular point-in-time in their journey. And constantly updating that content based on where that person is in their buying cycle.

"Have they been educated enough? Have they been on-boarded properly? Are they becoming a real advocate for our brand? Have they purchased from us? Are we treating them the right way? Greater personalisation is going to be huge.

"The best way to get all of this stuff happening is investing in your knowledge in marketing automation, and deeply understanding your customers.

"Customer-first content for 2017 and beyond is going to be huge. And this is of course going to impact with the changes that are happening within advertising, with everything being activated by our voice. That's coming quickly with the releases that *Amazon*, *Google* and *Apple* are making at the moment.

"Push marketing is just not going to cut it any more. We need to be personalising, nurturing and investing in customer-first content."

21) Improve your click through rates – Dan Petrovic

And of course nowadays, as Olga touched upon while she was talking about the importance of *Facebook* – how your prospects experience your brand doesn't start and end on your own website.

One place where people are likely to be introduced to your brand is in *Google*'s search results. And Dan Petrovic, founder of *Dejan SEO* is encouraging businesses to think about that initial interaction, and making it more likely for searchers to click.

Dan says: "One thing I want everyone to do in 2017 is to improve their click-through rates.

"*Google* looks at a variety of user behaviour signals, and these are split-up into two areas.

> *"If you expect a click through rate of 10% and you're getting a click through rate of 5% then you need to investigate why that's happened."*
> **DAN PETROVIC**
> *@dejanseo*

"I think most people are concerned about what people do on your website, but there's also the element of what people do before they land on your website.

"This is the click-through-rate between the search results towards your site. And it is influenced by a variety of factors that I think a lot of people are not considering when gauging how *Google* decides what site is popular, and what website is a user's choice.

"For this reason I recommend to go into *Google Search Console* and download all your available *Google* search traffic data, and observe the click-through rate graph by viewing your averages on each regular graph position.

"What you do with this data is look for anything that might be a deviation from what you'd expect.

"If you expect a click-through rate of 10%, and you're getting a click-through rate of 5%, then you need to investigate why that's happened. You can also calculate the expected clicks and decide where you're losing traffic and where you're gaining traffic.

"This will give you two things. Firstly, it will make your website more attractive. And secondly, it will give you the ability to A/B test your search snippets and implement schema to make them more attractive to click on.

"At the end of the day, if all else fails, you've gained more traffic with exactly the same ranking position, which is a wonderful thing to have."

22) Focus on your conversion funnel – Jeff White

Another man keen on getting more out of the same traffic is Jeff White from *Kula Partners*.

Jeff says: "Our top tip is around conversion optimisation.

"We've found for a great number of our clients that we've been able to conduct a really great analysis of what's going on beyond the surface of the site by looking at heatmaps and visitor recordings.

"You're able to get a great analysis of where people are stumbling on your site and where they're getting hung up in the conversion funnel.

"When you're looking at visitor recordings you can see people are filling in forms on your site and how they're going about doing that.

"We've been able to conduct a really great analysis of what's going on beyond the surface of the site by looking at heatmaps and visitor recordings."
JEFF WHITE
@brightwhite

"It's a really powerful tool for developing an understanding of where your site is working, and building a hypothesis of where you should be testing, so you can begin analytical testing and other types of split-tests, aiming to improve the conversion rate of your website."

[Editor's note: Remember to sign-up for your 2-month free trial of Hotjar's business plan as part of the 'Digital Marketing in 2017' book bonuses available at DigitalMarketingRadio.com/book]

23) Engagement and conversions on your website – James Bavington

For James Bavington, Director at the marketing agency *StrategIQ*, it's about engagement as well as conversions.

James says: "For me it's going back to basics a little bit. It's essential to get the website right and concentrate on engagement and conversions to maximise the marketing efforts being put into it.

"I might sound obvious to some people, but it's just amazing just how many businesses are still not doing this correctly.

"Fast and cheap hosting is available for everybody. SSLs are pretty much free now. And using tools like *HotJar* you can make informed decisions to underpin the marketing that you're doing.

> *"Get the website right and concentrate on engagement and conversions to maximise the marketing efforts being put into it."*
> **JAMES BAVINGTON**
> *@bavington*

"We're also having a lot of success with video at the moment. It's just really important to ensure when traffic is landing on the website that we're engaging with people and converting them.

"The actionable tip is to get buy-in from your development team. If they're engaged, and page speed and installing these tools is part of their ritual and routine, they'll support you in your efforts."

24) Tap your existing customers for new leads – Michael Kamleitner

Of course there are many benefits to engaging more with

your prospects and customers. For Michael Kamleitner from *Social Listen*, existing customers can be a wonderful source of new leads.

Michael says: "My advice has worked for us in the last year and hopefully will work next year, and it's very simple: Tap your existing customer base as a source for new high quality leads.

"How do you do that? Just by asking them for direct referrals or for reviews.

"What do I mean by direct referrals? Well it's very easy. Hopefully you will have some existing happy customers. They are a great source for new referrals and leads.

> *"Cultivate a deep relationship with your customers from the beginning."*
> **MICHAEL KAMLEITNER**
> **@_subnet**

"Don't be afraid to ask them straight – 'who else in your network and friends could be a happy customer for our service?'

"I guarantee you, if they are indeed a happy customer they will come up with some great referrals for you that should be easy to convert.

"Of course this works best if you cultivate a deep relationship with your customers from the beginning. If you haven't talked to your customers since they signed up last year, that will probably be an awkward situation!

"Therefore, I would also advise that you stay in contact, and foster deep relationships with your existing clients. You'll then have the opportunity to ask for referrals."

25) Test multiple offers at the point of exit intent – Chris Dayley

Finally, to conclude this chapter on customer journeys, Chris Dayley from *Disruptive Advertising* would like to encourage you to intervene, just as a visitor intends to leave your website.

Chris says: "One thing that I have been getting really excited about lately is exit and overlays.

"When someone is mousing over to 'x' out of your site, you should give them a pop-up with a high-funnel offer to try to encourage them to sign-up for your email distribution list.

"Some people have really negative feelings about these, because it can sometimes be construed as a way to manipulate people, or obtrusive in the site experience

"You've got to test multiple offers to find out what your visitors are going to respond best to."
CHRIS DAYLEY
@Chrisdayley

"But these are things I've seen to be very effective when I've been testing them recently with a variety of different clients. Especially if you have a site where people aren't going to be coming back frequently.

"So, if you're running PPC ads or any kind of advertising to a landing page for example, if you're going to lose your traffic on exit, you may as well give them a high funnel offer like a free e-book or some kind of free offer that they can sign-up to, to try to capture some information, letting you remarket to them later.

"I'm a huge fan of testing different offers at this stage. Because when people are intending to exit your site, there may be something that they could be really interested in at that point. But you've got to test multiple offers to find out what your visitors are going to respond best to."

Chapter 4: Customer Journeys – summary

- It's time for personalised campaigns – focus on the journeys of single buyers
- Get to know your buyers almost as well as you know yourself
- Use marketing automation with thought, to deliver a highly personalised experience
- Seek to optimise your off-site brand experiences and conversion rates too, such as click-through rates from search engine results
- Utilise heatmaps and visitor recordings from services like *HotJar* to enhance your on-site conversion rates
- Maximise the performance of your website before spending too much on paid traffic driving activities
- Tap your existing customers for new leads
- Test multiple offers at the point of exit intent – especially on landing pages for paid traffic

5 EMAIL & AUTOMATION

As Alita touched on in the previous chapter, alongside understanding precisely who your customers are, you need to try to deliver as personalised an experience as possible to each and every person that interacts with your brand.

But just because you wish to deliver a personalised experience, doesn't mean that you can't automate many of your marketing activities.

26) Use IFTTT & Zapier – Andrew McCauley

For Andrew McCauley from *AutopilotYourBusiness.com*, automation is key for him in 2017.

Andrew says: "With the introduction of all these tools like *IFTTT* and *Zapier*, it's really becoming an amazing playing field – you can automate a lot of the tasks that you do manually now.

"A lot of the tasks you've always wanted to do are probably available now through some of those apps. If you're not automating some of the tasks that you do on a regular basis, I think it's a really good time to do that now.

> *"You can automate a lot of the tasks that you do manually now."*
> **ANDREW McCAULEY**
> *@andymac71*

"Whether you're automating your content creation, automating some of the outreach that you're doing with influencers and journalists, all that can be automated.

"And these tools [*IFTTT* and *Zapier*] are some of the most powerful things that are available to us.

"I think 2017 is all about automation and making sure that you're not doing any manual work unless you have to."

27) Build your email list – Mike Allton

Something that certainly can be automated as well is the growing of your email list. And that's what Mike Allton, Founder of the *Social Media Hat* sees as being highly important in 2017.

Mike says: "What became clear over 2016 is that businesses and marketers need to own the land that they're building on. This is critical. Specifically when you're talking about social networks.

"This year we saw popular networks *Blab*, *Vine*, and others completely close down, leaving their users and communities to having to start over elsewhere.

> *"My renewed focus for 2017 is in building my email list."*
>
> **MIKE ALLTON**
> **@mike_allton**

"Email is more important than ever. When you're able to get your reader's email address and communicate to them, you keep full ownership and control over the experience.

"My renewed focus for 2017 is in building my email list and community, particularly through online courses and more digital downloads.

"Other businesses and marketers can continue to publish great articles and blog content to drive new and larger audience. But that should be supplemented with specific types of content that is gated behind an email subscription."

28) Your customers are not all the same – Matthew Turner

And as part of those email sequences, Matthew Turner from *SuccessfulMistake.com* highlights the importance of not treating all of your customers the same.

Matthew says: "My tip is very much piggybacked on the

work done by the likes of Ryan Levesque [*AskMethod.com*] and Scott Oldford [*GoInfinitus.com*].

"You shouldn't be 'shoehorning' people into the same bucket, because different people take different journeys. Scott Oldford always talks about having a customer on a sidewalk, a slow lane or a fast lane."

"There's no point in trying to sell high-ticket products to somebody who's not in the fast lane. In the fast lane, they're ready, they're primed. People in the slow lane, they need more nurturing. So do exactly that: nurture them over time.

"There's no point in trying to sell high ticket products to somebody who's not in the fast lane."
MATTHEW TURNER
@turndog_million

"My tip for 2017 is simply to look at your customers differently. They're not all at the same point on their journey.

"Put them in different places, speak to them in a way that's going to convert them to the next level. Over time you will get them to the promised land – which is those high ticket products."

29) Categorise your subscribers – Danny Ashton

Someone who's been having success with categorising his subscribers is Danny Ashton, Founder of *Neoman*.

Danny says: "I wanted to talk about what we're doing in our agency and what I've been doing over the past six months, preparing for 2017.

"Getting that obsession with your list. Every piece of content, every activity must align with getting someone's email. You won't get a real return unless you do that.

"The big one is making sure you've got the right tools. I used to use *AWeber* and now I use a tool called *Drip*. It makes the whole job for someone who's not techy like myself really simple on how to speak to different people.

> *"Getting that obsession with your list. Every piece of content, every activity must align with getting someone's email."*
> **DANNY ASHTON**
> *@dannyashton*

"Also – one big thing to think about is to make sure you tag stuff up when you do get a subscriber. Maybe a blog post, maybe *Facebook Ads*, maybe *Twitter*. You need to know exactly where your subscribers come from.

"Maybe I'm just a bit simple, but it's taken me about eight or nine years to get my head around those things. But once you do, things start to fit into place and then you can start scaling and investing in bigger pieces of content, and bigger volumes of advertising. And it's quite fun as well!"

30) Focus on behaviour and psychology to classify your personas – Michael Bonfils

Michael, Bonfils, Founder of *SEM International* is digging deep into why website visitors behave as they do.

Michael says: "My big digital marketing strategy for 2017 is to focus on behaviour and psychology in order to classify your personas for better content-based attribution channels. And I know that is a lot to look at!

> *"Focus on behaviour and psychology in order to classify your personas for better content based attribution channels."*
> **MICHAEL BONFILS**
> *@michaelbonfils*

"There is a book called *The People Code* by Dr Taylor Hartman, and it classifies people by motive, and by personality groups that you can then put into your personas to help you make incredible attribution-based digital marketing strategies."

It appears that digital marketing in 2017 is about understanding people just as much as it is about building systems.

31) Create emails that are worth talking about – Tom Tate

To finish off this chapter – Email and Automation – we're going to return to email, and specifically to what to include in those emails. Discussing that is Tom Tate, Product

Marketing Manager at *AWeber*.

Tom says: "Unsurprisingly my top marketing tip is to go back to the basics with email marketing and consistently send emails that are worth talking about.

"What I mean by that, is send a message that's not only going to make your subscriber's day, but be so noteworthy that he or she feels inclined to forward it to a friend or mention it to a co-worker.

"My number one step around this, if you really want to implement this strategy, is to take time to understand your email subscriber persona.

"Craft your emails as if you're writing those emails to one person. The inbox is truly a personal space, so make sure you are writing to the person and the human being on the other side.

"This applies to one-time broadcasts, promotional emails, automated emails. Whatever it is that you're sending.

> *"Craft your emails as if you're writing those emails to one person; the inbox is truly a personal space."*
> **TOM TATE**
> ***@tnrt***

"Write personal emails that give subscribers what they want and emails that are unique, and you will absolutely stand out in the inbox in 2017."

[Editor's note: AWeber have been kind enough to offer a 3-month free trial of their email marketing service to all readers of 'Digital Marketing in 2017'. Register for this and other bonuses at DigitalMarketingRadio.com/book.]

Chapter 5: Email & automation – summary

- Utilise tools like *IFTTT* and *Zapier* to automate your workflow
- Build your email list – own the land that you're building on
- Don't try to sell your 'high ticket items' to someone who's not ready yet, have a 'nurture bucket'
- Track exactly where your subscribers are coming from to measure the success of your various referral sources
- Improve your understanding of behaviour and psychology in order to classify your personas
- Craft your emails as if you're writing to a single person

6 HYPERTARGETING & ADVERTISING

Many businesses have no need or desire to target international business. In fact, most businesses are local in nature.

It's therefore very important that these sorts of businesses are highly efficient when it comes to reaching out to prospects. This chapter is dedicated to being as laser-targeted as possible when it comes to attracting the optimum audience, whether it's organic or paid.

32) Take personalisation to the next level – Joe Apfelbaum

For Joe Apfelbaum from *Ajax Union* a big part of being hyper-targeted is being highly personalised.

Joe says: "Marketing is always changing, what worked yesterday will not work today. What works today might not work tomorrow.

"One of the most annoying things about marketing is the lack of personalisation. When you get an email that is clearly not intended for you, it's a waste of time, money and resources.

"2017 is the year that we take personalisation to the next level. With the new data that we have on consumers and technology that lets us identify prospects – and only market to the relevant personas – we will be able to get people the value they deserve and have our marketing dollars spent more efficiently.

> *"Now is the time to take personalisation to the next level and create better results for your business and your prospects."*
> **JOE APFELBAUM**
> *@joeapfelbaum*

"You will see more marketing automation tools that will combine personalization from big data with smart AI algorithms that will tie-in factors like current events and special conditions.

"If the weather changes, we won't need to promote those coats that were set to go out. The smart computer software will be able to know what is going on, and send out campaigns that make sense.

"All-in-all, the more targeted you are with your goals, the more likely you will be able to accomplish them. Now is the time to take personalisation to the next level and create better results for your business and your prospects."

33) Think about how you can reach a local audience – Michael Fleischner

For Michael Fleischner from *Big Fin Solutions*, digital marketing effectively in 2017 is all about getting local optimisation and local intent right.

Michael says: "Especially with mobile, mobile search, everything is changing so rapidly with artificial intelligence starting to find its way in.

"The key right now, to anyone who has a business or is doing business online is to think about that local audience and how are they reaching the local audience. Are they optimising their website and other digital assets around local?

> *"The key right now to anyone who has a business or is doing business online is to think about that local audience."*
> **MICHAEL FLESCHNER**
> *@mfleischner*

"Whether it's content that's focused on a local market or a local area, or whether it's local directories, which have obviously come full-circle from years ago from an SEO perspective, the reality is that people are looking and shopping locally.

"If they can find a product or a service provider in their local area, they are much happier with that selection. If companies can focus on local and local intent, I think they'll have a great 2017."

34) Make sure that all your local data is correct – Grant Whiteside

And for businesses that do have a local presence, Grant Whiteside, Founding and Technical Director at *Ambergreen* shares that it's all about controlling your data.

Grant says: "I reckon one of the next battles we're going to see on internet search, where it will be won or lost is on the high streets and in the retail parks. This is all about getting your local presence sorted everywhere.

"This isn't just about *Google*. This is about *Bing* and *Facebook* and *Foursquare* and *Yelp* and other new sites and social platforms.

> *"one of the next battles we're going to see on internet search where it will be won or lost is on the high streets and in the retail parks."*
> **GRANT WHITESIDE**
> **@ambergreen_says**

"Make sure that your opening hours and your stock control and things like that are all as correct and consistent as they possibly can be.

"Because there's nothing worse than providing a terrible user experience. People turning up at the store and you're closed when results online said you would be open. Or your stock is not actually available when it says otherwise on the web.

"There is an opportunity to draw all these things together. It's going to be very much mobile based, data driven. Set up some measurement protocols to try and understand how offline and online work together.

Try using vouchers and managing the information from your CRM system and your email, and offline mail drops.

"If you can gather a better picture about why people want to come to your website, then you have a better idea about what you should be amplifying through your content.

"Through auditing your local search base, you'll find places where there's inconsistencies and poor reviews. There's a different sort of message that you can put out there. There's a great chance to put all these things together.

"And from a coding perspective, use structured data wherever possible because *Google* wants you to do this, and you want to be in *Google*.

"I think it's great to see that the knowledge graph that you're seeing [in *Google*] is pulling more and more third party data, structured data. It's pulling all this information together.

"And for multiple businesses with multiple locations – large brands – they're going to have to think about how they own that search base and provide relevant but unique enough content to that local audience as well.

"Content at scale might be a daunting task and a costly investment, but for many, it will be the difference between whether they can provide that space and own that space –

not only on the internet, but on the high street and in the retail parks as well.

"This is about drawing the whole local presence together in the first place. And understanding about how you win at that game."

35) Invest in a location management platform and clean up your data – Stephen Kenwright

Stephen Kenwright, Director of Search for *Branded3* agrees that managing your local presence isn't something that can be overlooked in 2017.

Stephen says: "I'm talking specifically to people in retail, people with physical locations. This year coming is going to be the last year that having physical locations is an unfair advantage.

"My best tip for the next year for anyone who has a physical business, is they need to invest in a location management platform. They need to clean up their data."
STEPHEN KENWRIGHT
@stekenwright

"I think what you'll have seen over the past couple of years is having that physical presence meant pulling people in via listings thanks to [*Google*] Venice and the Local Pack. It has been too easy for a while.

"My best tip for the year ahead, for anyone who has a physical business, is they need to invest in a location management platform. They need to clean up their data.

"They need to own all of the information about them on the internet. And that's not just on their own website. That's on directories, on *Facebook*, on every single platform they can get hold of.

"When voice search is coming (and will come in the next couple of years) you've only got one chance to give the right answer. Owning your data and being as clean as possible with that data is my best tip."

36) Try connection-based social advertising – Kamila Gornia

Next we move on to reaching the right people using the power of connection-based social advertising, with Kamila Gornia from *KamilaGornia.com*.

Kamila says: "My tip for 2017 is that entrepreneurs have to start using more connection-based social advertising, particularly *Facebook Ads*.

"I mean, not using ads as a means-to-an-end. A lot of people struggle with advertising when they don't see an immediate ROI. I beg to differ.

"I tend to work with entrepreneurs who are, or want to be thought leaders. And for people like this, impact is key. Connection is key. Without people knowing who you are, connecting with your story, and following your message, you have no impact, and no business.

"You can use Facebook Ads strategically to share your message: livestream, uploaded videos sharing your message, and then run ads to those videos to enhance their natural viral potential. Sometimes great content just needs a little push.

"Send lead generation ads for people to get into your back-end funnel. But you send them to people who have already engaged with you."
KAMILA GORNIA
@kamilagornia

"Once that's done, send lead generation ads for people to get into your back-end funnel. But send them to people who have already engaged with you. This gives them the feeling that you're 'everywhere' and they therefore connect more, engage even more, and see you as the authority."

37) Bid on impressions instead of clicks on Facebook – Andrew Foxwell

Andrew Foxwell from *FoxwellDigital.com* also had an interesting perspective for those advertising, or thinking about advertising on *Facebook*.

Andrew said: "I recently heard from *Facebook*, that of those people on *Facebook*, only about 60-70% of those users would show up in an action-based marketing objective. i.e. click and engagement.

"My big strategy that I'm going to be using moving into 2017 is for my low-funnel retargeting traffic, *Facebook* fans or previous customers. I am bidding for impressions versus bidding for clicks.

> *"I am bidding for impressions versus bidding for clicks."*
>
> **ANDREW FOXWELL**
> *@andrewfoxwell*

"This has been working very well in most of my e-commerce accounts, which is the type of work I do. It's targeting a larger proportion of the audience and bringing sales to our clients as well."

38) Use dynamic keyword insertion for paid campaigns – Calin Yablonski

Another way to improve the effectiveness of paid campaigns is to synchronise the experience between the ad and the landing page. That's something that Calin Yablonski from *Inbound Interactive* has been working on.

Calin said: "We do a lot of work in the legal sector, especially in *Google* search and conversion rate optimisation. And what we're seeing year-on-year is a continuous increase in the cost-per-click associated with those campaigns.

"This year, brands really need to start to focus on taking control of their marketing, and doing more extensive testing for things like their landing pages.

"We see a lot of really great results from dynamic keyword insertion as well as testing other elements on pages.

"I would recommend that if you're not doing things like dynamic keyword insertion for landing pages where your cost per click is quite high, then I would suggest it is something that you investigate.

> *"We see a lot of really great results from dynamic keyword insertion"*
> **CALIN YABLONSKI**
> *@calindaniel*

"This dynamically inserted content is taken from the query that someone is searching for. The process adds that phraseology to the headline of your ad copy as well as the headline on your landing page. For most of our clients we have found that we get really great results from it."

Chapter 6: Hypertargeting & Advertising – summary

- Work on identifying prospects and only market to relevant personas – aim to vastly improve your ability to personalise your content
- Focus on how you can be more effective at targeting a local audience
- Make sure that all your local data is correct – avoid customers experiencing incorrect information about your business online
- If you have a retail business with multiple locations, invest in a location management platform
- Use Facebook Ads strategically to advertise to people who have already interacted with your content
- Test bidding for impressions versus bidding for clicks
- Use dynamic keyword insertion to synchronise the experience between the ad and the landing page

7 CONTENT MARKETING STRATEGY

Delivering business solely though paid marketing activities doesn't take advantage of all the free traffic generation opportunities.

Content marketing is a way to build you and your business's status as a leading authority in your industry. It encourages people to interact with, and share your thought leadership.

It also builds brand recognition. The more that people interact with the content you produce, the more likely that they'll remember you and what you do when they're considering making a purchase decision in the future.

39) Invest more in content than you currently are: satisfy Google – Eric Enge

Someone completely sold on the necessity to invest more in content is Eric Enge, Founder and CEO of *Stone Temple Consulting*.

Eric says: "My top tip is to invest in more content then you currently are. I think that this is a good tip for almost everybody.

> *"My top tip is to invest in more content then you currently are."*
> **ERIC ENGE**
> *@stonetemple*

"With all of the investments that *Google* is making in machine learning, what they're getting better and better at is understanding what makes a good page, and a good user experience.

"From my perspective, that means they're going to be looking a lot at content quality, and the ability of your content to satisfy the breadth of needs that a user has when they arrive on a given page.

"If users arrive on a page on your site which is about one particular product, they're going to want to have a complete experience. So the investment in the content you put there, and the user experience they have on that page is going to be well worth the money."

40) Content marketing triple play – Mark Traphagen

So investing in content marketing is key. But what kind of content do you need to be producing? Mark Traphagen, Senior Director of Brand Evangelism at *Stone Temple Consulting* explains.

Mark says: "Building content is becoming more cost intensive if you're going to do it right. You can't do sloppy content anymore – it's not worth doing as it doesn't get attention. Nobody reads it, nobody shares it and it doesn't provide any value.

> *"You can't do sloppy content anymore."*
> **MARK TRAPHAGEN**
> **@marktraphagen**

"If you're going to invest in content, it's going to be expensive, time-consuming but it's going to be worthwhile. My strategy is to go for something that I call the 'triple play'.

"You've got to be producing content that does three things. Firstly, SEO value, You've got to have content for *Google*.

"Secondly, content that will build your brand value and reputation. Something that makes people sit up and take notice, remember your brand, and makes your business name come to mind when they're ready to buy your product.

"And thirdly, content that will generate leads.

"None of that is new, but I encourage people to work with content that does all 3 things at the same time. So keep that triple play in mind for your content in 2017."

41) Document a content marketing strategy – Rebecca Lieb

Rebecca Lieb, Analyst/Strategic Advisor at *RebeccaLieb.com* thinks that not enough businesses are documenting their content marketing strategy.

Rebecca says: "We're still seeing that close to 70% of marketers don't have a documented content strategy, but nearly 100% are committing to content marketing.

"Without that documented strategy, you don't know what goals you're trying to achieve, how to measure your progress and what tools and resources you need. You have to get this stuff down on paper, or into the cloud and document it.

"I think one reason that marketers don't have a strategy is that they fear that somehow if they write this stuff down, it becomes like tablets – it's immutable and can never change.

"You can always change your strategy – change, adjust and amend the strategy as your needs and goals evolve. But you need a strategy before you start exercising the tactic."

"You can always change your strategy – change, adjust and amend the strategy as your needs and goals evolve. But you need a strategy before you start exercising the tactic."
REBECCA LIEB
@lieblink

42) Organise your content to support the buyer journey – Alex Tucker

Alex Tucker, an inbound marketing and demand generation specialist at *PracticeWeb.co.uk* emphasises the importance of organising content to support the buyer journey.

Alex says: "What I would encourage you to do is to is to think about your prospects – whatever your product or services – as being in one of three states.

"At the first state they're not even going to know they have a problem, with completely unidentified needs.

"At the second state they may have identified a problem, but they don't have the time or money to do anything about it. They might not have the information, or just not care enough. It might just not be that urgent.

"The third state would be that they are actively looking for something.

> *"Organise your content so that it supports the buyer journey."*
> **ALEX TUCKER**
> *@tuckera*

"For the first state, the content that we need to provide is just our most useful content. We need content that makes their life easier.

"Then at the second state, this is all about social proof. The best thing we can do is to bring people closer to us when they know they have a problem, but they don't want to do anything about it. For this, have a strategy of case studies, testimonials, ratings, reviews and all those good things.

"Then, the final state, where they're actively seeking a solution, is content that proves value. In the consumer world, this is our offer, our sample. In the B2B world it might be your free consultation for our professional services clients.

"If you can optimise those three content types to draw people through your marketing funnel, you're going to be getting much higher engagement with your content marketing.

"The final tip is to have a look at the channels. *Google* has published an interactive tool based on the data they have about what channels are working in various industries.

"If you search *Google* for '*Google customer journey*', you'll find the interactive tool from *Google* that is going to tell you which channels people are using as they move through the buyer journey.

"Match those to the content types that you need to produce and optimise your content marketing efforts for conversion all the way through."

43) Editorial planning – Natalie Sisson

For Natalie Sisson, the *Suitcase Entrepreneur*, planning your content is a key element of success over the coming year.

Natalie says, when asked about her digital marketing tip for 2017: "For me it is to get your content marketing and editorial calendar all planned out this month.

"It sounds like a big deal, but jot down each month what you're going to cover on your podcast, your blog, your platform and your emails.

> *"Get your content marketing and editorial calendar all planned out this month."*
> **NATALIE SISSON**
> *@NatalieSisson*

"The minute you have your things set out for the year – what you're going to be talking about – you can create everything else in flow with it.

"You know what promotions you're doing, you know what social media you're going to be putting out, you know how your content is going to flow, what you're going to be writing about in emails.

"I have a free calendar and I just think that this is THE most important thing to be able to do. Just put it into your template, set up your year ahead and feel in control and focused."

[Editor's note: Natalie has kindly provided a link to the editorial calendar that she uses for all 'Digital Marketing in 2017' readers. Simply register for this and all other bonuses at DigitalMarketingRadio.com/book]

44) Prune your content – Kevin Indig

But content marketing success isn't just about producing more and more content. Kevin Indig from *Kevin-Indig.com* actually advises on getting rid of some of your existing content.

Kevin says: "My top tip is called 'pruning'. It is a method, which is comparable to cutting off the weak branches from a tree, to make the whole tree stronger. That's how you can imagine it.

> *"My top tip is called 'pruning'. It is a method, which is comparable to cutting off the weak branches from a tree."*
> **KEVIN INDIG**
> **@Kevin_Indig**

"Why would you want to do that? Firstly, to improve your overall [organic search] rankings.

"Second, not to become [*Google*] Panda food. Because the Panda algorithm targets thin pages [in terms of content].

"Third, to save your users from seeing bad content through search. Because we all know how sensitive bad user experience is. Furthermore, this will save your *Google* crawl resources.

"So, how would you do this? First of all you have to identify those weak pages. Indicators for those pages could be user signals such as bounce rate, time on site, pages per visit, and of course, traffic (no traffic, no lifetime traffic over a certain timescale, or no rankings at all). You want to review which of your pages are performing poorly.

"You can use an analytics tool for things like click-rate and use your rank tracking tool, matching that against all your pages.

"With the last step, you should set those weak performing pages to *no-index*, or you could simply exclude them from being crawled. Either that or you could improve them and their content, and provide a better user experience.

"Your final option is to consolidate those non-performing pages with well-performing pages in the hope to rank for more keywords, and ranking higher in general."

So it's not just about producing content in 2017, it's about managing all of your existing content more effectively.

45) Consider the topical mesh – Laurent Bourrelly

Another man keen on managing content – both on-site and off-site – and the links between those pieces of content is Laurent Bourrelly from *LaurentBourrelly.com*.

Laurent says: "Today, keywords are not enough. You have got to beyond keywords with concepts, ideas and topics. But that is still on-page SEO.

"With on-page SEO, people have figured out that it is not enough to just talk about keywords. You've got to consider a whole bunch of other words surrounding the keyword, to make the page stronger.

"What we found out is that beyond the page, the content on all the related off-site pages also count for a lot of the power of the page. How pages are linked together with semantic affinity is the key.

> *"How pages are linked together with semantic affinity is the key."*
> **LAURENT BOURRELLY**
> *@laurentbourelly*

Laurent then suggested that certain elements of SEO software were further ahead in France compared with the rest of the world.

"In France" he said, "we already got a bunch of tools. It is already becoming best practice and you are still missing one part of the solution.

"But if you speak French you can try to find the information, otherwise you have to wait a few weeks until we come out and explain it to you.

"But basically, you can experiment yourself with trying to surround the page with other pages that relate to the topic. Beyond topical SEO, I call that the topical mesh.

"Topical SEO is more about on-page SEO and topical mesh is everything surrounding the page."

So an intriguing hint at what's working for Laurent. What's surely important to bear in mind is the necessity to be aware of your competitor's content marketing activities and what's working for them. And you intend to write new content, ask yourself: 'Is my proposed new content going to add real additional value to what already exists on the web?'

46) Link to long-lasting content – Mark Pack

Mark Pack, Associate Director at *Teneo Blue Rubicon* has a relatively straightforward tip that helps with bringing context to your content for search engines.

Mark says: "My top tip is to do with link building. Lots of people quite rightly still pay a lot of attention to link building, but often forget that just as you're creating and winning new links, links rot at the other end.

"Think carefully about how long-lasting the page or the piece of content that you're linking to is likely to be around."

MARK PACK

@markpack

"As you're getting new links in, you're losing links out the back end. Particularly when you're giving external links out, getting that touch of authority that search engines like *Google* really love.

"Think carefully about how long-lasting the page or the piece of content that you're linking out to is likely to be around.

"If it's not likely to be long-lasting, you're better to link somewhere else. So that search engines in six months' and twelve months' time don't find a broken link, they still find a functioning link."

47) Use disavows at keyword level as well as site-wide – Laura Hogan

Talking about links and the impact that they can have on your online success, Laura Hogan from *Rice Media* advises readers to not to underestimate the value of *Google*'s Disavow Tool.

Laura says: "Since the launch of Penguin as part of *Google*'s core algorithm, we're seeing the impact of Disavow files taking positive effect on rankings in days (rather than months).

"My action is to use Disavows at keyword level, as well as site-wide. With granular Penguin, you'll see the impact of a Disavow just focusing on one area which has dropped, rather than the whole site."

"Since the launch of Penguin as part of Google's core algorithm, we're seeing the impact of Disavow files taking positive effect on rankings in days"

LAURA HOGAN
@lauralouise90

So quite a technical recommendation by Laura. However, it is a recommendation that could be extremely useful indeed if your site previously received a lot of organic search traffic – and you're currently experiences ranking challenges on *Google*.

48) Personalise your outreach – Andy Drinkwater

Next up Andy Drinkwater, an SEO Consultant at *iQ SEO* provides his opinion on how to improve your outreach.

Andy says: "I live on *Twitter*, and one of the big areas that I see people complaining about all of the time is outreach, and the emails people get on a daily basis... sometimes many, many times a day.

"It's very clear that there is still a lot of confusion as to what makes good outreach – and I don't think that good outreach necessarily needs to be complicated.

"Lots of people will just send a blanket email out and hope that they get some sort of feedback, some sort of response from it.

"In actual fact, the one thing that is missing is the personal journey that comes with outreach, and that is where you pick up the phone and make contact with somebody.

"The one thing that is missing is the personal journey that comes with outreach, and that is where you pick up the phone."
ANDY DRINKWATER
@iqseo

"I've been doing this for several years now with great success. There's universities, there's colleges where you wouldn't just send a blanket email. You have to do a little bit of digging to find out who you need to talk to.

"Don't just assume that by sending an email that they're going to be interested in what you've got to say, because the chances are they won't.

"Have something ready that is going to be of interest to them. Don't just assume that you're automatically going to gain a link from somebody, or that you're going to start building rapport with someone over email. Because that's probably not going to happen.

"I would certainly say, don't be afraid to pick up the phone. Do a little bit of digging around, do a little bit of research. Find out who you need to be talking to.

"Don't just automatically go in there all guns blazing and say 'I want a link'. Proposition yourself as a resource. Don't just go in there and say 'I want something for my website'. Pick up the phone and don't be afraid to talk to people."

Chapter 7: Content Marketing Strategy – summary

- Invest more in content than you currently are
- Think SEO value, brand value and leads – prior to having content produced
- Document your content marketing strategy before focusing on the tactics
- Organise your content to support the buyer journey
- Put together an editorial calendar, with your content plan for the year
- Prune your content – determine your underperforming content and consider de-indexing or combining underperforming pages
- Research how your proposed content compares with content that already exists
- Try to only link out to evergreen content, so that your

links are still valid in the future
- Try focusing on just one area of your site with the Disavow tool
- Don't be afraid to pick up the phone when conducting outreach

8 WHAT TO PUBLISH

But of course, *how* to publish and *when* to publish isn't much use unless you know exactly *what* to publish, *how* to structure that content and *what* precisely to include in that content.

49) Pay attention to what people want, not what we think they want – Janet Fouts

Janet Fouts from *JanetFouts.com* advises to pay attention to what our prospects want, not what we **think** they want.

When asked to summarise her digital marketing tip for 2017 Janet says: "Paying more attention to what people really want instead of pushing out what we think they want.

"If we take a mindful approach to our audience, and really look at what it is they're looking for, and figure out how we can get there.

"We use things like *Google Trends* to find out what they're looking for, listen to conversations out there, and talk with people instead of talking to them.

"Paying more attention to what people really want instead of pushing out what we think they want."
JANET FOUTS
@jfouts

"I think that's going to be crucial. We expect a lot more from our marketers [in 2017] and so we've got to step-up and supply that."

50) Stop trying to game the system – Kris Reid

Upping our game is certainly something that Kris Reid from *Ardor SEO* agrees with.

Kris says: "Anyone that knows SEO in the slightest hears the terms 'White Hat' and 'Black Hat'. Black Hat describes the naughty stuff that master *Google* disapproves of and 'White Hat' is the squeaky clean stuff that doesn't always get results.

"Every year *Google* gets bigger, more powerful, and has way more data to back up their search results. It's becoming that much harder to game the system.

"My advice: stop trying to game the system and provide what *Google* wants. What *Google* wants is great user experience through superb content.

"Creating super-high quality content that engages with users will not only up your rankings through an increased click-through rate and a lowered bounce rate, it will also make all of that traffic even more valuable – as it will increase conversions.

"Stop trying to game the system and provide what Google wants. What Google wants is great user experience through superb content."
KRIS REID
@Ardor_SEO

"My suggestion is to go through *Google Search Console* (previously called *Google Webmaster Tools*). Find the highest ranking pages and go through *Google Analytics* to find the paths that users take through your website, where they are dropping off and not converting, and focus your energy there. Work on these pages to make them more descriptive and more engaging. Have users 'dying to take action' to become customers."

51) Do we deserve to rank? – Lexi Mills

And we need to be honest with ourselves about the quality of the content we're producing. Lexi Mills (*@leximills* on *Twitter*) says that it's important to ask ourselves the question, 'Do we deserve to rank?'

Lexi says: "In bygone days, many tried to dupe *Google* by building fake links. Then the industry was focused on building real looking links. The majority then graduated to strategies that would encourage natural links. But that's not enough with the introduction of machine learning.

"We will need the full ripple effect of signals to continue to optimise well. Meaning, we have to execute ourselves and strategies with integrity, because the machines are already smarter than us – and this is only going to grow.

"Integrity underpinning the structure of optimisation and business imprints on the internet, and gives me immense hope for the future of this landscape. Because if we have to ask ourselves what we need to do to deserve to rank, by default we are forced to interrogate our business proposition.

> *"If we have to ask ourselves what we need to do to deserve to rank, by default we are forced to interrogate our business proposition."*
> **LEXI MILLS**
> *@leximills*

"The best content and PR stories I have seen and worked on have always come from this place, promoting the decisions companies make and why. There is clearly still some work to be done around brand dominance and filter bubbles for this to flourish, but one step at a time."

52) Focus on your core target audience and stand out! – Marcin Chirowski

For Marcin Chirowski from *GrowthTurn.com* it's about really understanding who your target audience is.

Marcin says: "My top tip for 2017 is go back to basics and just focus 100% on the challenges and aspirations of your core target audience before you start creating anything.

"Before you start creating any new content, focus on your core target audience.

"Before you start creating any new content, focus on your core target audience."
MARCIN CHIROWSKI
@MarcinLondon

"This may sound simple and silly, but as you know, SEO and content are becoming increasingly difficult if you don't stand out, yet often we see brands creating bland content.

"Currently, everyone is producing content. We are fighting for user attention. Attention is something you've only got a few seconds of, so brands have to really stand out. And the way to do that is to be 100% focused on the target audience."

53) Understand the 'language of lack' – Mike Mindell

Mike Mindell, Founder of *Wordtracker* has been in the business of keywords for many years. And for him, it's all about understanding the specific phraseology that people are more likely to use in certain scenarios.

Mike says: "What I want you to do is think about when you're entering a new market. Think about a really big idea. And that idea is this...

"In order to really want something, you first have to

perceive that you don't already have it.

"And I know that sounds little bit philosophical, but just think about the idea again. In order to really want something, you first have to perceive that you don't already have it.

"Imagine I have a cup of coffee in front of me. Say a Starbucks, a Chai latte, and I'm taking a sip from it. I'm enjoying it. And you come over to me and say 'Mike, do you want a Chai latte?' I'm going to say no thanks, I don't need another.

"The same thing would apply if I had my *iPhone 6*. I've got an *iPhone 6* in front of me and you turn round and say 'Mike, would you like an *iPhone 6*?' I'd go 'well, no. I don't want one, I already have one.'

"So in order to **really** want something, I have to perceive that I don't already have it.

> *"The language that you use to express that lack is what you put into engines like Google."*
> **MIKE MINDEL**
> *@wordtracker*

"Now if you said to me 'do you want an *iPhone 7*', I might look at my *iPhone 6* and go, you know what, I don't have an *iPhone 7*, I think… depending on the features and the battery life and all this stuff – maybe I do want an *iPhone 7*.

"I didn't know before, but maybe I do now. And here's the really important point: the language that you use to express that lack is what you put into engines like *Google*. Two trillion times a year, 107 billion times a month. The language you use to express that lack is what you put into Google.

"So wouldn't it make sense that next time you go into a niche market, to sell your products or service, to actually look at what people are searching for, and what the lack is, and the language that they're putting into that search box?"

54) Estimate the potential reach before producing the content – Cosmin Negrescu

Cosmin Negrescu, Founder and CEO of *SEOMonitor* believes that it's essential to know the potential reach of your content before you come close to deciding to produce the content.

Cosmin says: "There are lots of trends like mobile-first and video and so on. These are great things, and we should definitely use them to enhance the content we produce. But sometimes we forget that distribution is far more important than producing the content itself.

"Instead of tackling many channels, just try to focus on finding the one channel that will bring the majority of the growth."
COSMIN NEGRESCU
@ncosmin

"My tip is to always try to estimate the reach and the impact of any acquisition initiative, that's before putting the time and money into producing the content.

"That way, you validate whether it is or it isn't worthwhile putting the effort in.

"Most of the time [if there isn't enough keyword volume] you won't cancel the initiative. You'll just get creative in finding new ways to reach more people with your message.

"It's not about being completely accurate. It's more about being thoughtful, going through the process of estimating the impact.

"Another thing – there's also this rule that applies to any fast growing company. It's been found that a single distribution channel brings about 70% of their growth.

"Instead of tackling many channels, just try to focus on finding the one channel that will bring the majority of the growth.

"The thing is that there's a golden age of each channel. Remember *Facebook* five years ago? What happens there is that a company can gain a lot if they find the right point in the lifecycle of a channel.

"You can still get a lot of ROI from just focusing on a single channel. That's because a single channel can still have a large audience – and perhaps you've identified a place without much competition. So I'd say before 'mobile first', we should think 'distribution first'."

55) Answer questions – Ann Smarty

Another source of content ideas should be your audience's questions says Ann Smarty, Founder at *SEO Smarty*.

Ann says: "Most people [most of your audience] want to find answers to their questions. How well you are answering them on your website is how well you are doing [from an organic search perspective].

"You can see this now on *Google* as they feature the best answers, and their website, in a quick answer box.

"Try searching for a question and you will see a quick answer box in the search results, giving those publishers more opportunity to get clicks and traffic.

> *"Most people want to find answers to their questions – how well you are answering them on your website is how well you are doing."*
> **ANN SMARTY**
> **@seosmarty**

"There are two really cool tools that help you find the questions that people are typing in the search box. Firstly *serpstat.com* (try searching for any word and it will show you all the searches that people do for that term). And *answerthepublic.com* (same way – search for your word and it will show you a mind map of all the questions that people tend to type)."

56) Produce visual data-driven content on a weekly basis – Nadya Khoja

With all this great research that you're conducting on the content that you should be writing, just because you're finding phrases to include, doesn't mean that you should only be publishing the written word.

Nadya Khoja, Head of Marketing for *Venngage* shares her belief that visual content needs to be a significant part of your strategy.

Nadya says: "I'm pretty confident that visual content is going to take a big hike in 2017.

"We already know that visuals like infographics and videos are 30% more likely to be seen and consumed than most text-based articles, and the majority of our communication is visual.

"Businesses are not only focused on functionality now, but when people look at a business it is not only about functionality, it is more about aesthetic. Is it a cool business to do work with?

"Marketing in the B2B industry is moving towards visual, specifically animated graphics. Static images are just not as engaging as they used to be.

"I've noticed a lot more marketers pushing to include graphics in their content – and video in their content. Not just static graphics, but moving graphics. Such as bigger GIFs with data moving in and out of the canvas.

"On top of that, we need to be more consistent when we're producing this content.

"One really great visual a month is no longer good enough. You need weekly visual content that is jam-packed with data-driven insights, and also beautifully designed.

> *"One really great visual a month is no longer good enough, you need weekly visual content that is jam packed with data-driven insights."*
> **NADYA KHOJA**
> *@NadyaKhoja*

"In order to do that and implement that strategy I recommend starting out looking at your top performing content and trying to repurpose that into engaging visuals first.

"You can do that by pinpointing the main takeaways and tips that are highlighted in that content, and any relevant points or data. Then, using some type of tool or hiring a freelancer on *Upwork* who can quickly transform that information into a compelling video or motion graphic.

"After, if you've tested out the strategy and it works for you and your audience by repurposing your content, you can start implementing it on all of your content as you move forward. And I think that will boost engagement in 2017."

57) The content marketing mother test – Emeric Ernoult

Let's end this chapter by hearing from Emeric Ernoult, Founder & CEO at *Agora Pulse*, who believes that there's one very simple way to determine whether or not your content is good enough. He also has some advice on why you shouldn't spend all of your time behind a computer.

Emeric says: "The next piece of content you write – make it go through the mother, or the best friend test.

> *"Too many marketers stay in their ivory tower thinking about marketing strategies, tools, tactics and the latest object on the marketing field."*
> **EMERIC ERNOULT**
> *@eernoult*

"Is it a piece of content you would send to your mother and be proud about it? Is it a piece of content you would send to your best friend and be proud about it? Is it a piece of content you would send to the influencers in your ecosystem and be proud about it?

"My second piece of advice, which I learnt as a start-up founder, is to get out of the building and talk to customers.

"I think that too many marketers stay in their ivory tower thinking about marketing strategies, tools, tactics and the latest object on the marketing field. And they forget about knowing what the customers want, need and say about their products and services.

"With marketing and other jobs that are not directly customer facing, getting out and talking to customers can be very insightful."

Chapter 8: What to Publish – summary

- Pay attention to what our prospects want, not what we think they want
- Stop trying to game *Google* – what *Google* wants is great user experience through superb content
- Ask yourself what you need to do to deserve to rank
- Focus 100% on the challenges and aspirations of your core target audience before creating content
- Understand the specific phraseology that your target market is likely to use when expressing the potential 'lack' of your product or service
- Estimate the potential reach before producing the content
- Focus on your single best distribution channel
- A source of content ideas should be answering your audience's questions
- Produce data-driven animated gifs on a regular basis to augment your written content
- Set your content the 'mother test'
- Get out and about and talk to your customers face-to-face

DAVID BAIN

9 THINK HUMAN

Carrying on from Emeric Ernoult's final point in the last chapter, this chapter emphasises the increasingly important human element of digital marketing in 2017.

58) Keep the customer at the centre of your business – Steve Linney

For Steve Linney, Founder of *eMRKTNG*, a marketer should start at the customer and work backwards.

Steve says: "For me, it's concentrating on the customer being at the centre of your products and the centre of your business. You should start at the customer and work your way backwards.

"It's easy to get caught up on why you think your product is fantastic or your business is fantastic, but you can forget to concentrate on the benefits to the customer.

"You need to create amazing customer experiences. And this doesn't necessarily need to be anything major, or over-the-top, or have a big budget.

"It just means customer experience, customer care and customer respect running through your entire organisation. And with that, it's personalisation, but personalisation in that people understand the individuals behind the brands.

"Because in this day and age, people buy the person as much as the brand. And simple things such as a thank you email from your CEO when a purchase is made can make a big difference. It's just small subtle changes.

"It's concentrating on the customer being at the centre of your products and the centre of your business."
STEVE LINNEY
@stevelinney

"Finally, it's turning a negative into a positive. How you deal with customer complaints can make or break a business.

"There's a good quote from Jeff Bezos from *Amazon* that in the physical world you might tell six people if there's an issue. Online, it can get out to six thousand people really quickly. It's how you respond to any complaints in a professional, timely and thoughtful manner that matters."

59) It's about the passion and humanity that you bring to your online activities – Trevor Young

And for Trevor Young from *PRWarrior.com* it's about the passion and humanity that you personally bring to your online activities.

Trevor says: "Focus more on what I call the right side brain of social media and content marketing.

"The left side is the tools, the analytics, and the data, the templates, the systems, and the processes. That's all important of course. But to cut through the clutter, to resonate with people, you need to ask yourself 'what degree of uniqueness can I bring'?

> *"To cut through the clutter, to resonate with people, you need to ask yourself 'what degree of uniqueness can I bring'?*
> **TREVOR YOUNG**
> **@trevoryoung**

"The right brain to me, aside of content, is the concepts and the stories, the ideas, the collaboration, the insights, the connections you make. And the passion and the humanity that you bring to all of your online activities."

So both sides of your brain are required for content marketing in 2017!

60) Humanise your content – Mojca Marš

Mojca Marš from *Super Spicy Media* is someone else who's going to be focusing on humanising things in 2017.

Mojca says: "This last year I've worked with a lot of clients and something that has worked well, and in 2017 is only going to get more powerful, is humanising content.

"Share as many personal photos as possible, tell your story. Communicate, and try to connect on a personal level with your audience. Because when you do that, you immediately differentiate yourself from other competitors.

"When you visit *Facebook* and you open up your newsfeed, you can see all these brands that are pretty much promoting in the same style, most of the time.

"When you try to be different with more personal content – personal stories, and personal photos, that's when you stick out.

"When you try to be different with more personal content, personal stories, and personal photos, that's when you stick out – so be different."
MOJCA MARŠ
@mojcamars

"Be different to most of your competitors, and people are going to remember you by your personality and connect with you more – and purchase anything you have to offer.

"The personalisation and humanisation of your company would be my number one tip for 2017."

61) Give people a reason to promote your content by including them – Kevin Gibbons

For Kevin Gibbons, Managing Director at *BlueGlass*, a great opportunity is to get influencers involved in your content, so they'll be much more likely to promote it when it's published.

Kevin says: "My tip is tapping into egos – trying to get people involved in your content so that they can help promote it.

"If you do things like interview 100+ experts on a show [referring to the show that produced this very book!], you've straight away got profiles behind all those people that will help you to promote that content. It really helps to make things go much further.

> *"Get people involved in your content so that they can help promote it."*
> **KEVIN GIBBONS**
> *@kevgibbo*

"I've tried this in a few campaigns – I've interviewed agency owners (and again it helps because it's not just my opinion that's being shared), clients and vloggers, and tried to get them talking about the right things.

"The more that they're a part of it, the more they're

naturally going to share and look to promote it – because they're invested in it.

"Trying to get someone to promote a piece of content they've had nothing to do with is tough. You need to give a really good hook and angle.

"Creating and promoting something that they've been involved in is so much easier, because they're going to promote themselves – and help you at the same time."

Collaboration – 62) Andrew and 63) Pete

Another couple of gents who agree that working with others is absolutely key in 2017 are Andrew and Pete from *AndrewAndPete.com*.

They say: "We want to talk about something which has worked really well for us for the past few months, which will also be our focus for next year, which is collaboration.

"With collaboration, we feel like it's one of the quickest, easiest and cost effective ways to quickly grow your audience. And not just grow an audience, but grow an audience full of your target market.

"The best thing about collaboration is often it's free. And it works across pretty much every platform. You can do *Facebook Live* take-overs, you can have *Facebook* guests coming in, you can have *Snapchat* takeovers, *YouTube* video collaborations. There's so much you can do and it's the best way to grow your audience.

"Specifically, for small businesses it can be super-powerful.

It's so untapped in the small business world. You can also do some great stuff with B2B. Look for other businesses, look for people in your industry, look for potential influencers. It can even work for B2C.

> *"The best thing about collaboration is often its free, and it works across pretty much every platform."*
> **ANDREW AND PETE**
> *@AndrewAndPete*

"For example, if you're targeting university students, why not just find the most popular student in school and get them to do an interactive *Facebook Live* video with your product. Just pay them with *Greggs* vouchers!"

64) Take the complex, make it simple, then teach it – Chris Marr

Chris Marr, Founder of the *Content Marketing Academy* believes what most marketers need to focus on is honing the skill of taking the complex and making it simple. And then teaching it.

Chris says: "I believe that as marketers, as business owners, based on what I've observed over the past year, is that we get far too distracted by all the shiny new objects, application software – it's that shiny red ball syndrome.

"I think that going into 2017, what we need is more focus and more discipline around the principles of great communication and great marketing.

"Reading what everyone else has to say – some amazing ideas – stuff that honestly I'd never even heard of before, far more advanced than probably I'll ever get to.

"The important things are, why does this all matter to business? How does this grow businesses? How does this make a difference to our audiences? How does this make our customers better people? How does this change lives?

"We need to all stop trying to look smart. We need to stop trying to tell people what we know about certain subjects and stop trying to give everyone everything we know about a certain topic. Because as soon as we start to try to look smart, we start to look stupid.

"What my mission is, what I'm all about, what I teach my audience and my customers about, and I want business owners and marketers to think about going into 2017 is how can they take the complex, how can they take the shiny new stuff, how can they take their ideas and concepts which may be complex, and turn them into something simple.

"It comes back to impacting and changing lives. And the only way that we are able to do that properly … is to take the complex and make it simple."
CHRIS MARR
@chrismarr101

"How can they communicate in a way that takes that complex issues, the stuff that people just don't understand – and communicate it to [their audience] in a way that helps them to understand.

"Not just what it is, but why it matters to their business. In other words, how can they be great teachers? How can they teach these complex issues to people, that helps them to understand why it matters.

"I think that's the skill that most marketers are missing. And I believe that it's a skill that matters the most as well.

"It comes back to impacting and changing lives. The only way that we are able to do that properly – and to do it at scale, and to do it in a way that impacts as many people as we can – is to take the complex and make it simple.

"And communicate in a way that makes people understand why it matters to their business, and in turn helps them to grow their businesses too.

"That's my tip for 2017 for all digital marketers out there and for all business owners out there, to focus on being great at communication. Don't just try and transfer all your knowledge about a certain subject. Think about how you can teach it in a better way, that helps people to understand, and therefore impacts your own business."

Chapter 9: Think Human – summary

- Start at the customer and work your way backwards
- Make sure you bring your own passion and humanity to your online marketing activities
- Include your own personal photos and personal stories as part of the business brand identity
- Give people a reason to promote your content by including them in the content
- Collaborate with influencers and leverage their popularity

- Take the complex, make it simple, and then teach it

10 AFTER HITTING PUBLISH

So far we're heard a lot about defining your content marketing strategy, what type of content to produce, what to include in that content – and the tone of that content.

But we haven't thought much about how we're going to ensure that the content is seen by as much of your target audience as possible.

65) Focus on the distribution side of content marketing – Mark Asquith

For Mark Asquith, Founder at *Excellence Expected* and kind writer of the foreword of this very book, it's a concern that too many people focus on the production of the content rather than the distribution of it.

Mark says: "Everyone talks about content marketing, but

clients generally only do the content bit – we need to get them to focus on the marketing bit. You need a strategy or marketing plan for each piece of content.

> *"Everyone talks about content marketing, but clients generally only do the content bit."*
>
> **MARK ASQUITH**
> *@MrAsquith*

"My key actionable takeaway is to repurpose as much as you can and focus on pushing it out to the channels that matter."

Wise words from Mr Asquith there. Don't get trapped spending the vast majority of your time producing, with little time or budget left to promote.

66) Smart repurposing – Colin Gray

For Colin Gray, Founder of *The Podcast Host*, a content promotion plan should be part of the content marketing process.

Colin says: "The coming year for me is about building far more engagement, and at the same time, trying to build a whole lot more [audience] reach.

"Obviously that's a bit of a difficult combo – deep engagement takes length, it takes depth and attention.

"Tailor your media to particular mediums and particular people. That helps you engage with individuals, but it does not achieve that reach.

"What I'm doing is implementing a lot more design and structure. And I know that sounds general, but that's a digital marketing tactic for me because I find that structure tends to put off creative people.

"They don't want structure and all those things to tie them down, but I find that structure gives me a whole lot more freedom and a whole lot more creativity.

> *"Structure gives me a whole lot more freedom and a whole lot more creativity."*
> **COLIN GRAY**
> **@thepodcasthost**

"The way that that works for me, is that every bit of content I plan, I'll plan it out in bullet points, and I'll use that structure.

"I'll plan to write a blog post and record a video based on the same topic – and it's funny how often that video will turn out to be better than if I hadn't planned it.

"Because I've already written a blog about it I've processed that bit in my head, and because I've structured it, it lets me break it down into four, five, six different sections. What I can end up with is taking the audio from that video series and releasing it as a podcast episode.

"You've got the podcast which is long and engaging and draws people in, and you've got the text there which also engages people – and that's where the reach is.

For me, that structure allows smart repurposing, releasing it on different mediums, and using the power of those mediums individually."

67) The content waterfall – John Lee Dumas

John Lee Dumas from *EOFire.com* shared a very specific content promotion sequence that he starts each day with.

John said: "I consider myself a content marketer first, so I'm going to give [my tip] a content marketing strategy focus.

"It's the content waterfall. I think anybody can develop their own content waterfall. I'm going to give an example of mine.

"First, I choose a quote that inspires me. Then I write an email about it and send that email out to my list. I then take that same email that I just created, and put it on *LinkedIn* publishing, and then put it on *Medium* publishing.

> *"Anybody can develop their own content waterfall."*
> **JOHN LEE DUMAS**
> *@johnleedumas*

"Then I go into *Snapchat* and I do a little JLD rant on that exact quote. Then I take all of those individual *Snaps* and I copy them over to *Instagram Stories*.

"After that I take the *Snaps* and put them into a 1-minute

video, posting it on *Instagram video*. Then that same one-minute video goes onto *Facebook* as well.

"I use the content within the email that I wrote earlier to paste below the *Instagram* post and the *Facebook* message.

"That's a content waterfall that I create that allows me every single morning before 9am to do more content marketing than most entrepreneurs do all day!"

68) Ask your customers about your marketing – Daniel Burstein

For Daniel Burstein from *Marketing Sherpa*, getting that reach means talking to your own customers about your marketing activities.

Daniel says: "My tip is to question the very motivations of your marketing. That's something we call, at *Marketing Sherpa*, 'customer-first marketing' – are you putting your customers first?

> *"think about the small ways you can put your customers first."*
> **DANIEL BURSTEIN**
> *@DanielBurstein*

"One quick piece of data first: we conducted a study with 2400 consumers here in the US and we asked them what they thought about companies' marketing.

"And the unsatisfied customers (the customers who were

unsatisfied with a company), the top thing they said was the company does not put my wants and needs above its own business goals.

"Think about the small ways you can put your customers first. Whether it's telling customers 'here's reasons why you should buy, but hey, this product isn't for everyone – here's a few reasons why you shouldn't'

"Segmenting prior to sending to customers serves you best.

"We have a construction software company – HCSS – that we interviewed: they changed their entire marketing to be around content marketing and saw over 50% growth in their revenue.

"Because their content marketing wasn't about their products, it wasn't about the thing they wanted to sell. It was about their customer's problems. Which in this case, was about recruiting people to their construction companies."

Chapter 10: After Hitting Publish – summary

- Repurpose what you can, and focus on the distribution side of content marketing
- Think about how you can distribute new content on multiple platforms, yet still creating content that is native to each platform
- Build a smart content distribution system that you can quickly and easily replicate on a regular basis
- Focus on solving customer problems at all stages in the content marketing cycle

11 SOCIAL MEDIA & PR

The web used to be a place where you published, and others consumed. There wasn't any direct interaction between publishers and consumers.

Now that's turned 180 degrees. Customers expect interaction now. And if they don't get it, it's likely that they'll go somewhere else.

Chapter 11 looks at how you and your business can take full advantage of social media and PR in 2017.

69) Focus on your core audience – David Shaw

For David Shaw from *DavidMarkShaw.com*, it's not about the numbers, it's about focusing on your core audience.

David says: "I want (particularly) small businesses to understand they should stop spending a lot of time on social media building what I call a manufactured audience – where they've been getting all of these follows and likes just for the sake of it.

"Lots of social media gurus have told them that you've got to build this big audience; and they're not actually focused on people who are interested in their business and their content.

"When they look at their metrics it shows that their social media sucks, as the majority of it is just not being seen.

"We've seen the algorithms coming together over the last year or two and what [social media networks] are really doing now is straining out a lot of the content. That content's not getting consumed. It's not getting the likes or shares that it requires.

"I want people to understand… they've got this manufactured audience. They really need to clear it out and start focusing on smaller audiences that are genuinely interested in your content.

"It might mean a cleansing of your social media – focus on quality followers who are actually interested in what your business is trying to provide in terms of value."

"Focus on quality followers who are actually interested in what your business is trying to provide."

DAVID SHAW
@Davidmarkshaw

70) The four "Ts" of social selling – Ollie Whitfield

Ollie Whitfield from *Creation Agency* meanwhile believes that it's important to utilise sales skills on social media.

Ollie says: "I think of my work in social selling as a hybrid of sales and marketing. What that really means in my space, is when I get cold calls, it's an interruption, it's annoying. I don't trust the person. I find it really annoying. And I'm definitely not the only one who thinks that. So I've coined my ideological 'four T's of social selling'.

"The first one is **trust**, the new way to do it is not to barge in and call me at 9pm in the evening. Try to reach me in a way that lets you build some kind of trust.

"The next stage is **timing**. A lot of the time, when people buy, it's because it's the right time for them to buy. If you try and make them buy when it isn't the right time, then the chances are, they won't.

"Third out of four is **turnover**. You need to build real business from your social selling activities.

> *"Nobody knows what's right. We can only find out what's right by testing."*
> **OLLIE WHITFIELD**
> *@ OllieWhitfield_*

"Lastly and probably the most important, is to **test**. Particularly in my line of work. Social selling is quite a new thing, so maybe not everyone *gets* the best way how to do it.

Maybe we don't even know yet. So the reason for 'test' in this four-word suit, is nobody knows what's right. We can only find out what's right by testing."

71) Less automation on social media – Heather Porter

For Heather Porter from *HeatherPorter.com*, it's essential that we interact natively on each social media platform.

Heather says: "My top tip is less automation on social media. This allows you to do more cross-channel promotion.

"What I mean by that is, you might put up a video and a longer written post on *Facebook* for your business.

"If you're launching something, grab the permalink for that particular *Facebook* post, go over to *Twitter* and tweet about it – but in the native language of *Twitter*.

"Then go over to *Instagram* and tell your story on *Instagram*, which is also promoting that particular post over on *Facebook*.

"After, go over to *LinkedIn* and put an article up there, giving a couple of the top points that you're discussing in that post over on Facebook, so you're cross-promoting.

> *"Speak in the native language of the social platform that you're using."*
> **HEATHER PORTER**
> *@businesshostess*

"The key is this... instead of having one post that goes out across all your channels saying the same thing, with the same media, your literally speak in the native language of the social platform that you're using."

72) Personal branding through social media – Sam Hurley

Sam Hurley, Managing Director at *Optim-Eyez.co.uk* has been super-successful over the past couple of years at building his own personal brand on social media.

Sam says: "I was able to quit employment and start my own business purely through *Twitter*, *LinkedIn* and *Facebook* – and I still don't have a fully functioning website.

"I break down [how I did this] into 5 steps:

"Step 1 – decide who you are and what you want to provide as an individual. That is the most important step.

"Step 2 – choose no more than three relevant social media platforms and assess how you can make a big difference on those networks. Really take the time to research your competition and dedicate yourself to provide more value than [others] appear to be providing.

"I was able to quit employment and start my own business purely through Twitter, LinkedIn and Facebook."

SAM HURLEY
@Sam___Hurley

"Step 3 – it's fine to look up to influencers, but be unique in everything you do – including your visual branding, messaging and tone. Just be different because there's really no point in copying anybody else.

"Step 4 – build rock-solid relationships and take the time to respond to people. It's something I've done from the start, and its helped me tremendously. 10% of those people will be able to help you get to where you want to be – this is critical.

"Step 5 – once you've built these valuable relationships, do not lose track of them. It's a great idea to use social CRM software, like *Nimble*, and marketing automation platforms, such as *Wishpond*, which allow you to build and nurture email lists that can eventually turn into sales."

73) Growth hacking PR – Josh Steimle

In relation to how you're perceived online, Josh Steimle from *MWI* shares his own PR strategy for 2017.

Josh says: "My tip has to do with how to include PR within your digital strategy. I recommend that you go old-fashioned and build real relationships. Here's how I do it…

"Follow 20 journalists on *Twitter* that you wish would write an article about you. Turn on the mobile notifications so you get an alert about everything they post so you can really stalk them!

"Whenever they tweet something you like, heart it and retweet it. And do this for about two weeks. This takes some time, but the reason this works is because nobody else does it.

"Then look at which journalists have followed you back after two weeks. Reach out to them and ask these questions: 'What stories are you working on right now?' and 'Is there any information you need, or any sources your trying to connect with?'

"And when they get back to you – some of them will get back to you, some won't. If they respond, you help them. If you can't help them, you tell them what you're an expert at, and you say 'hey, if you're ever writing a story on what I'm an expert on, let me know and if I can't help you out, I'll know others who can.'

"Follow 20 journalists on Twitter that you wish would write an article about you, turn on the mobile notifications so you get an alert about everything they post so you can really stalk them!"
JOSH STEIMLE
@joshsteimle

"For those you've been able to help, you do this one or two more times. Once you've been able to help a journalist one or two times, you reach out and say 'can we have a phone call or a *Skype* call, can we meet in person?' (if you're close by them)

"Once you meet them, just get to know them a little bit – at no point in this process ask them to write a story about you – but get a phone call with them – make it really short –

around 10-15 minutes, and then you just keep helping and keep communicating. That's it.

"Most people ask 'okay, but where do I get the article?' Don't worry about it, don't even think about it. If you do what I suggested, if you provide this type of value to journalists, they will get to know you.

"Journalists, like anybody else write about people that they like and trust. And if you get on their trusted list – trust me they're going to end up writing about you whether you pitch them or ask for that article or not. And once you get that article published, that's great for your SEO. It's an old fashioned tip but it works great for your digital strategy."

Josh certainly walks the walk when it comes to this recommendation as he's had articles published in the likes of *Forbes*, *TechCrunch*, *Mashable* and *Time*. Check out the full interview that I did with him over at *DigitalMarketingRadio.com/josh-steimle*.

74) Stay on top of trends & make social & SEO play well together! – Lukasz Zelezny

Talking about leveraging other marketing activities to assist with your SEO, Lukasz Zelezny from *Zelezny.uk* always tries to have one foot in SEO, and the other in social media.

Lukasz says: "For me, SEO (which has always been a big love) and social media, which is like a new young brother, they should be playing together in the same team.

"First of all, all the new things that are up-and-coming in SEO like AMP pages, featured snippets, and things like

SSL, building a responsive site, having good load time etc. These things always need to be spot-on.

> *"Make SEO and social media play together for the same team."*
> **LUKASZ ZELEZNY**
> *@LukaszZelezny*

"Every time *Google* says 'hey, we are implementing something new', even if some webmasters may not understand why they are doing this (like the people complaining about AMP pages at the moment), you should still implement it. Because over the next year, you will say, 'oh my gosh, that was a good decision.'

"Then when you have this in place, go to social media to promote your content. There are tools like *Commun.it*, *Brand 24*, *Tweepy* and *Crowdfire*. All these tools and more help you automate the outreach and amplification of your content.

"That would be my advice for 2017. Don't forget about social media and how powerful it can be; and how much it can boost your fantastic content and SEO achievements. Make SEO and social media play together for the same team."

Chapter 11: Social Media & PR – summary

- Don't build a large, manufactured audience. Build a relevant, core audience
- Keep on testing to see what works. Nobody knows what's best for you and your business. We can only find out what's right by testing
- Spend less time automating on social media. Speak in

the native language of the social platform that you're using

- Build your own personal brand on social media by being unique and building rock-solid relationships
- Follow 20 journalists on *Twitter* that you wish would write an article about you and offer to serve – build real relationships with them
- Make SEO and social media play together for the same team – but don't focus on social media without getting your SEO right first

12 VIDEO & LIVE STREAMING

Since early 2015, live instant video broadcasting has grown exponentially. Services like *Meerkat, Periscope* and more recently *Facebook Live* have enabled anyone with a smartphone to broadcast live whatever they're doing, wherever they happen to be.

But just because it's easier to broadcast and publish video, should every business be involved? And if you are going to participate, what are the best ways to get involved? And what are the pitfalls?

75) Emotional intelligence & video – Saija Mahon

Saija Mahon, Founder/CEO at *Mahon Digital* believes that it's very important to know how your emotional intelligence fits into your overall digital marketing strategy as well as your video strategy.

Saija says: It's really important that as brands, or for the clients we have, that the stories we are trying to promote comes across in a meaningful way.

"Within digital marketing it's often all about data, big data and crunching numbers plus *Excel* sheets and working with tools.

"But sometimes we forget that behind all of those numbers, there are people who want to buy from our clients or from us. We therefore need to remember their emotions as well.

"The way to do that is focusing on video, which is a great opportunity for all advertisers and [agencies] as well.

"A *YouTube* channel is a great way to improve personal branding for free. And really get that personal message or brand message going, and start to develop your story, getting that story across to people.

"We do forget that behind all of those numbers, there are people who want to buy from us — therefore, we need to remember their emotions as well."

SAIJA MAHON
@SaijaMahon

"My top tip for 2017 is to craft your story, and start getting that out to your audience, engaging with your audience emotionally. Video is an amazing, growing way to do that and it doesn't need to break the bank either."

76) Promote your pre-recorded video with live video – Amy Schmittauer

Amy Schmittauer, founder of *SavvySexySocial.com* has been a prominent, successful video publisher for a number of years. And her tip for the coming year is to combine the power of live and pre-recorded video.

Amy says: "My biggest tip here is to remember what we are being given here on a silver platter. And that is the luxury of things like *Facebook Live*.

"We obviously have a big live push [in 2017]. The big thing is about taking advantage of that and sending people to where you want them to go.

"If you are thinking about starting a *YouTube* presence, then you should leverage things like *Facebook Live* to promote your content.

"If you are thinking about starting a YouTube presence, then you should leverage things like Facebook Live to promote your content."
AMY SCHMITTAUER
@Schmittastic

"We often build things and hope people are going to come. That's probably not going to happen in the early days. Especially in places like *YouTube*.

"This first 24-48 hours is going to determine whether or

not your video will be successful in the long-term.

"In that first few moments after your video is published on *YouTube*, take advantage of the organic reach you're getting by promoting on *Facebook Live*.

Get on live, talk to your audience, let them know that you just published something cool. Offer them more value and you will start to see a new way to push the traffic in the direction of all the videos you're going to be creating in 2017."

77) An evergreen, searchable video marketing strategy – Roberto Blake

A man who's experienced a lot of video success is Roberto Blake from *RobertoBlake.com*. Roberto's top tip for 2017 focuses around *YouTube* and video marketing in general.

Roberto says: "Number one, you need to have a strategy of evergreen, searchable content – that's going to be very useful as one of the most searched things on *YouTube* is 'how to…'.

"If you want to establish yourself as a subject matter expert, or demonstrate what your company does in terms of product or service, this is a really great foundation for you.

"Firstly, look at the 10 or 20 pain points that a buying customer has, and build a foundation of evergreen searchable content around that.

"Number two, create content that serves as a calling card.

"If you're an individual with a personal brand then you have to think about what your goals and objectives are – do you want to be a public speaker, get more panels, get more consulting clients?

"What type of content serves as a calling card to your client? Maybe that's not something that's evergreen – maybe it's something that you capitalise on in the moment, or with a trending topic that you speak on in an authoritative way that showcases your knowledge, skills or expertise.

"It could even be something that's micro-niche – for a very specific person, with the goals and intentions of getting the eyeballs of just one brand, or one specific person.

> *"Look at the 10 or 20 pain points that a buying customer has, and build a foundation of evergreen searchable content around that."*
> **ROBERTO BLAKE**
> **@robertoblake**

"Number three, community-based content. Once you have people in your ecosystem, you have to keep feeding them things that are valuable to them.

"A lot of the time, to do that community-based content, you should be curating through your audience, or even having them do participatory content in the form of *YouTube* live stream Q&As.

"It could even have static pre-recorded Q&As where you

have fielded information from your audience in the form of *Twitter* polls, *Twitter* questions or from a *Facebook Group*.

"Number four, video optimisation or SEO. I can't stress enough the importance of good titles, descriptions and tags. This needs to be focused around things that are searchable, but also things that trigger related videos on *YouTube*. The algorithm recently changed, and a lot of 'related videos' now come from user behaviour, based upon what they recently viewed.

"Make sure you use tags that aren't just one or two words, but phrases that can relate to other videos or topics.

"Some useful tools for this are *VidIQ*, *TubeBuddy*, *Keyword.io*, and the *Google AdWords* tool.

"Number five, in your content strategy make sure you are making what would be considered objectively to be good content. Content that has very clear value, at least on some level. Well produced – even if it's with a smart phone, try and make it stable, and make sure there's good audio. Make sure the viewer's experience is a quality experience."

78) Create your own video ads – Justin Deaville

And video is not just about producing content designed to be consumed via organic search. Justin Deaville, MD at *Receptional* shares that creating video ads can be quite cost effective at the moment.

Justin says: "My agency does quite a lot of work advertising on *Google*, and so I've been lucky enough to be invited to speak at various events.

"I thought I'd ask [representatives from *Google*] what their predictions were for 2017. Of course the first answer I got back was that mobile is still important. That's not really news to most people reading I'm sure.

"They also said that the number of desktop and tablet visitors are now both decreasing, searches are falling for both of those device types.

"Once I'd pushed that idea to the side, the one thing they were talking about was *YouTube*. They talked about how the number of people watching television versus online is about the same now.

"We spend as much time watching online videos as we do watching television. But the advertising dollars haven't followed.

"We spend as much time watching online videos as we do watching television. But the advertising dollars haven't followed."
JUSTIN DEAVILLE
@justindeaville

"It's actually quite cost effective to be able to advertise with video. And that's something *Google* wants to encourage. They want to get more people advertising on *YouTube*, so they're subsidising that and trying to make it easier for people to create video.

"The big problem is that people don't have the kit, the lighting and the sound equipment. So they've created the *Director app*, which is available on the iTunes store but not yet on Android (but that will be coming soon, I think).

"And that has got some ready-made templates, which are based around the kind of videos that are already successful on *YouTube*.

"It allows you to very easily add-in your own text, animations and sound, and all the things you would need to produce a really good quality video.

"It's aimed at much smaller businesses than you would expect, so it's worth checking out that *Director app* if you haven't yet advertised on *YouTube*.

"The second thing that's worth mentioning is that Google are subsidising the costs of production, because they've realised that making video can be expensive if you're doing it for the first time.

"Google will now send someone to come and create a video in your place of work, provided you're spending at least £350 or $500 [on AdWords]. They will do that for free in quite a few locations now.

79) You need to be using live video streaming – Peter Stewart

There are many more reasons why you should be incorporating live video as part of your digital marketing strategy thinks Peter Stewart from *PeterStewart.co.uk*.

Peter says: "2017 is the year you need to be using live video streaming. Stuff like *Facebook Live* and *Periscope* – those are the two big players – but there are probably about a dozen more similar services that you could get into.

"Just keep in mind to fish where the fish are, so don't get onto a platform where none of your friends, family, clients, customers or colleagues are. It's probably going to be *Facebook Live*, particularly when I tell you about what's happening there.

"Any live stream you do through *Facebook* is going to get into more news feeds than any other content that you put on *Facebook*. Much more than straight up links, text or pre-recorded video.

"Therefore, you're going to be shown to more people, and that means there is going to be a greater chance that they will be watching and interacting with you.

"Once people are watching *Facebook Live*, they are commenting 10 times more than on any other content.

> *"Once people are watching Facebook Live, they are commenting 10 times more than on any other content."*
> **PETER STEWART**
> *@TweeterStewart*

"You can talk directly with your fans, friends, colleagues, clients etc. And you can ask them questions, show them things, you can broadcast from different locations –

because of course it is on phone as well as your desktop.

"You can become a thought leader, show behind-the-scenes at an event or production line, or maybe even in your boardroom, letting viewers comment and help you in the decision making process.

"All of this is available now through *Facebook Live*. Also with additional software, you can build in other cameras, drones, *GoPros* – you can have a TV-like production from your desktop.

"2017 is the year that you need to just try it! You can do a private broadcast just to yourself – dip your toe in the water and see how it works."

80) Make live video evergreen – Ian Anderson Gray

Another fan of live video is Ian Anderson-Gray from *Seriously Social*. Ian believes that it's important to try to make live video evergreen.

Ian says: "Everybody seems to be talking about [live video] at the moment. Next year it's going to be even bigger, particularly as *Facebook* pushes hard with *Facebook Live*.

"Something I'm going to be concentrating on a lot in 2017 is producing regular, live video content – particularly on *Facebook Live*. But also looking on other platforms such as *YouTube* and *Periscope*, now that we can broadcast from our computers using multiple webcams.

"My particular focus is looking at how you can make live

video evergreen. I think with live broadcasts, we think a lot about the number of viewers we have. But many times we will have far more viewers looking at the replay, so it's making sure that the content you are producing is going to last for a long time.

> *"My particular focus is looking at how you can make live video evergreen."*
> **IAN ANDERSON GRAY**
> *@iagdotme*

"The live element is instant and it's a really great way to show the real you, and to have fun. You can bring in guests, and it's also a great way to boost that reach, particularly on *Facebook* because they notify all your friends and fans.

"I'm also going to be focusing on making the post afterwards – the text – really high quality. Adding in links and replying to comments, and doing that regularly."

81) Get good at repurposing video – Dennis Yu

Dennis Yu from *BlitzMetrics* thinks that a lot of SEO and PPC people need to start picking up video distribution as an addition skillset.

Dennis says: "For all of us that have done SEO and PPC for a living, to deal with text that we either write or get from others, what will you do about video?

"Video is what's driving traffic and conversions in mobile and social. And this is content that most 'content marketers' (who were previously 'SEO' people) just don't know what to do about.

"The key is that old-time SEO people have to work with the client to collect these videos, chop them up into snippets for social distribution on *Facebook*, and then 'boost' [advertise].

"If you're in-house, same thing. You won't be able to produce enough video in-house, so you have to rely upon processes that help your customers to generate video.

"I'm not talking about *Fiverr* or automated animation stuff. Customers are too smart. They see through cheap tactics.

"If your product or service doesn't generate awesome reviews naturally, you have to question whether you're in the right business. No amount of SEO or PPC witchcraft is going to work for you over the long-term."

"If your product or service doesn't generate awesome reviews naturally, you have to question whether you're in the right business."
DENNIS YU
@dennisyu

82) Turn real-world events into online experiences – Mike Bryant

If you think about it, you may well have existing offline content that you can turn into video and online content.

That's what Mike Bryant from *Page One Power* intends to be doing in 2017.

Mike says: "I want to focus on offline events and turning that into a real, valuable experience for attendees, speakers and vendors by turning these events into a live virtual conference too, or something that's published online quickly after the event.

"I challenge readers to focus on engagement and having real conversations that are one-on-one, providing a presentation that is interactive.

"You get that live feedback from the audience during the presentation, and have your people/team prepared to capture that interaction and broadcast it immediately. Make it quick and get it out to all your social channels.

> *"Focus on engagement and having real conversations that are one-on-one."*
> **MIKE BRYANT**
> *@MichaelRo22ss*

"Some of the other trends I'm seeing are live video, 360 degree video, virtual reality and augmented reality. You need to consider if these make sense for your brand in 2017.

"If you don't have content that can match up with that type of media, perhaps sit tight with that. Wait a little bit, be patient, develop the content first, then put it out on those platforms.

"My takeaway is a challenge to the readers: ask questions, get your voice heard, make sure that the audience know what your challenges are."

83) Do audio if you can't do video – Ilise Benun

Sometimes, for whatever reason, you might not be in a position to be able to produce video. If that's the case, Ilise Benun from *Marketing Mentor* advises you to give another medium a go instead.

Ilise says: "For the people who can't do video for whatever reason: either they don't want to do video or they don't know what to do, my suggestion is do audio instead.

> *"For the people who can't do video … my suggestion is do audio instead"*
> **ILISE BENUN**
> *@ilisebenun*

"Maybe it's an interview, maybe it's reading something aloud that you have written. And then you can post it on *YouTube* as a video with an image instead of a video.

"You can use automatic transcription to get the text and turn that into a blog post, or a series of blog posts.

"That's basically my little content marketing waterfall."

84) Master creating great audio before producing video – David Bain

But even if you are focusing on video, don't discount the importance of great audio. Many people get turned off watching videos on *YouTube* because of the poor quality of the audio.

And bearing in mind that I've hosted over 300 podcast episodes myself, I'd like to add my own tuppence of advice here too…

"In 2017 video content is becoming the norm. It used to be that producing your own videos was something that was fairly unique. But now that there are so many others doing it, you need to make sure that you are producing your videos at as high a standard as possible.

"It's now getting to a stage where people are looking for an excuse not to consume your content. If they don't like one aspect of it, they'll quickly lose interest and move on to someone else that's more enjoyable.

"Take the time to master the creation of great audio before producing video."
DAVID BAIN
@DavidBain

"One of the under-appreciated aspects of video is sound quality – including volume, pitch and background noise. If you can't get that right, that's a significant reason why people may not be watching your videos for long.

"So take the time to master the creation of great audio before producing video.

"It doesn't have to cost much. Purchase a USB/XLR combi dynamic microphone such as the ATR-2100 or the Samson Q2U. Purchase a simple microphone windshield and a swing desk stand for your mic and everything together will cost less than $100 (about £80).

"Then learn the craft of producing good audio. Speak 4 to 6 inches away from the microphone, with the microphone at a slight angle. And practice.

"When your audio is great, that's one reason that your content consumers will continue to engage with your videos in 2017, rather than preferring your competitor's content instead and never coming back."

Chapter 12: Video & Live Streaming – summary

- Start to develop your story and get that story across to people – don't hide behind a brand
- If you're publishing on *YouTube*, leverage *Facebook Live* to promote your *YouTube* videos as soon as you publish them
- Look at the 10 or 20 pain points that a buying customer has, and build a foundation of evergreen searchable video content around that
- *Google* are subsidising some of the cost of producing video ads for *YouTube* – check out what's available in your local area
- People are 10 times as likely to comment when

watching *Facebook Live* – leverage that interaction

- Enhance your *Facebook Live* post with more detail after your live session is over to make it more 'evergreen'
- Chop up your existing video content, publish it on *Facebook* and pay to boost your posts, continuing to test which content 'flies' best
- Turn real-world events into online experiences by shooting video at your own live events
- Commit to recording and publishing audio, if for whatever reason you can't do video
- Ensure that your audio quality is spot-on – even for video. Don't give discerning viewers a reason to switch off

13 REAL PEOPLE SKILLS

In chapter 9 we already discussed the necessity to add some humanity to the content that you're producing.

Here in chapter 13, we're going even further and encouraging you to work on those real people skills – even though you probably spend the majority of your time behind a computer!

85) Talk to your customers directly – Robert Brady

Robert Brady from *RighteousMarketing.com* has a background in PPC data analysis. Even so, he's started to focus on who his customers are and getting to know them better.

Robert says: "I think with as much power as we have in the digital world - analytics, link building, PPC, social media, video etc., it's easy to get lost from the fact that our customers and readers are real people.

"My strategy is to get back to your roots and focus on who your customers are and what drives them from an emotional perspective.

"The one actionable step that I think everyone should take this year is to get in touch with your customers directly.

"The one actionable step that I think everyone should take this year is to get in touch with your customers directly."

ROBERT BRADY
@robert_brady

"If you have someone that you work with who is in touch with those customers on a regular basis – your customer service reps for example, perhaps your sales team – go and schedule a 30-minute sit-down with them and interview them with questions.

"Asking them what are they are hearing from your customers can help you with your keywords. What's driving customers can help you with your ad copy, and your landing page copy.

"Have that interview, ask really hard questions. Record it, transcribe it and then use it in all of your materials. Because if you understand the people you're trying to reach better, everything improves."

86) Build up real relationships – Anton Shulke

Another man focused on building real relationships is Anton Shulke, a webinar expert from Ukraine.

Anton says: "My tip is a very old one. It is to build a relationship.

"It's impossible to build a relationship with everybody, so try and build relationships with influencers. To do that you have to bring them value.

"A personal relationship with an influencer is of value in itself, and I think that most of the time we don't treat it very seriously – I think that it is very important.

> *"It's impossible to build a relationship with everybody, so try and build relationships with influencers"*
> **ANTON SHULKE**
> *@anton_shulke*

"If you do influencer marketing – which you should do – go that extra mile and find out about your influencer, not just professionally but about their personal interests and hobbies."

87) Empathy – Jonathan Tilley

Personal Brand Strategist Jonathan Tilley from *JonathanTilley.com* encourages you to take the time to really understand why the people you interact with act in the way that they do.

Jonathan says: "My top tip is not a tool, it's not something you can grab. It's something that you feel. My 2017 tip is **empathy**.

"We do so much work marketing ourselves and marketing our businesses, sometimes it's all about 'us, us, us, us' when it should really be all about our client. Who are we working for?

"We do so much work marketing ourselves and marketing our businesses, sometimes it's all about 'us, us, us, us' when it should really be all about our client."

JONATHAN TILLEY
@JonathanTilley5

"Use tagging to keep that conversation going, and not just going in for the kill of the sale, but also holding their hand if you must.

"Make it all about them and putting their shoes on your feet, and walking around in their shoes and making the text, making the copy. And do the same when using whatever social media platform it is that they're using.

"Make them feel at ease at how they consume what you produce. Because we are inundated with so much content that you need to create content which is specifically for them and their needs, so much so that they feel there is a spy cam in their brain."

88) Be authentic – Evan Pettrey

For Evan Pettrey from *Valley Inbound*, 'authenticity' is key.

Evan says: "With all these amazing tools and technology and data that shrouds us today, we're seeing a lot of people that aren't being their true selves, they aren't being authentic.

"My tip is, as you're growing your business, as you're growing your audience, there is a natural tendency for some of us to try and be who we think our audience wants us to be.

"But in reality, audiences are smarter than ever. It's so easy to see who is being authentic and who is not. It's really important that we let people see who we truly are.

"Don't get lost trying to be somebody else, or the perfect person who has figured everything out.

> *"Don't get lost trying to be somebody else, or the perfect person who has figured everything out."*
> **EVAN PETTREY**
> *@EvanPettrey*

"We're all humans, we're all trying to learn as we go through this – especially in an industry that is so rapidly changing.

"We need to put ourselves out there and admit that there are times when we're going to make mistakes, or we do the wrong thing.

"But as long as we keep picking ourselves up and learning from mistakes, learning from the data and continuing to get better, that is what is really important.

"So keep building, keep hustling, but as you grow, stay grounded to your core – and be authentic."

Chapter 13: Real People Skills – summary

- Talk to your customers directly, and utilise the feedback to assist you with your keywords, your ad copy and your landing pages
- Build real relationships with influencers, taking time to understand things like their personal interests and hobbies
- Make your client feel so much at ease they almost feel like you have a spy cam directly in their brain
- Be authentic to who you really are, don't try to be perfect – people are much more likely to relate with the real you

14 INSIGHT

We hear the phrase 'test and learn' all the time, but how do we actually implement this and keep on incrementally improving what we do over time?

And with so much data available to you and your business, where do you possibly start?

89) Audience insights – Ben Oliver

Ben Oliver from *ID Collective* says you should begin your insight journey by taking the time to understand your audience.

Ben says: "My biggest digital marketing tip would be spending some time on audience insights.

"We spend so much time on the creation and reporting of content, we often overlook the audience we are supposed to be serving in the first place.

"Given how dynamic the industry is, and how quickly audience needs can evolve, it's vital to be conducting audience research every 6-12 months.

> *"We spend so much time on the creation and reporting of content, we often overlook the audience we are supposed to be serving in the first place."*
> **BEN OLIVER**
> *@BenOliverAus*

"Some tools I can recommend include *Facebook Audience Insights*. I particularly like the Page Like tab which provides insights into what other pages your audience follows.

"Also, *Minter*. This is a great analysis tool for understanding your *Instagram* audience.

"And *Affinio*. This is one of the most powerful audience insight tools I've come across, although sadly just for *Twitter* at the moment. *Affinio* allows you to analyze your *Twitter* audience (or other *Twitter* audiences) by placing them into tribes based on affinity. For example, within your *Twitter* audience there may be a sub-section that really likes vintage cars.

"By knowing this, you can serve more precise content, work with better influencers, better manage your media spend, etc. It's not a cheap tool, but one worth looking into."

90) Maximise your use of analytics – Glenn **Schmelzle**

For Glenn Schmelzle from *Marketing What's New*, there's so much data out there available for free, it would be a mistake not to use it.

Glenn says: "Recently we have seen an explosion in the number of ways that we can measure things. We can prove how prospects interact with us by reviewing their click patterns.

"It's just becoming *so* democratised and *so* cheap to be able to do cross-channel tracking, looking at user behaviour through heatmaps or polls, or live chat data.

"Taking session recordings, getting more video engagement information, matching user data so that you can see who has filled in shopping carts or joined your members area, or who you've cookied elsewhere.

"Form interactions, interactive widget metrics, page load times. Seeing now how people tap or swipe and scroll through pages. This is great data and I think that marketers need to stay up with this.

"I would encourage everyone to go onto their *Google Analytics* and go to the top right hand side. There is a grid button there, and that is where you can see some even newer tools.

"The good old saying, 'if you can't measure it, you can't manage it' is still true."
GLENN SCHMELZLE
@heyglenns

"In addition to *Google Analytics*, there's *Google Tag Manager*. But there's also *Google Data Studio*. That's a great tool for visualising and telling a story with very appealing reporting.

"My theme is to point out that the price of many of these things has dropped to zero. And it's now ultimately up to us to better utilise these tools.

The good old saying, 'if you can't measure it, you can't manage it' is still true, and now we can measure exactly what is working on our website. Get insights and make it an amazing experience for people who are visiting us."

91) Use the data inside your business more effectively – Matt Forman

Another man keen on evangelising the value of using data more effectively in businesses is Matt Forman from *Traffika*.

Matt says: "We're all awash and drowned with data everyday as digital marketers, but there are so many free tools, and there is so much low-cost computer power and solutions nowadays to help you make better use of that data.

"To give you a very simple example, within *Google Analytics* there are some simple attributes called *Custom Dimensions* that you can use to extend your analytics data.

"Just joining up simple things like your information from your CRM or point-of-sale system into your *Google Analytics* account really helps you get a much clearer clue as to who your customers are, and how [your customers] are behaving. Not just on your website, but offline as well. So you can start to create segments and understand behaviour based on all sorts of information.

"The other really exciting and powerful thing about doing that is you can then start to use this information for better targeted advertising.

"That could be via creating *Custom Audiences* in *Google* and using that in *Google Adwords*, or in *Google Display Network*. Or even using *Facebook*'s offline data API to push data into *Facebook*.

> *"Make much better use of data you already have."*
> **MATT FORMAN**
> *@mattforman*

"You can start to get very precise and specific with your advertising as well – which ultimately leads to a better customer experience, and a much better return-on-investment.

"That would be my top tip. Make much better use of data that you already have with some very low cost and free tools that are already out there, accessible to everyone."

92) The importance of digital marketing audits and when to do them – David Sayce

David Sayce from *DSayce.com* believes that although conducting regular audits may be perceived as the less glamorous side of digital marketing, regular audits build solid foundations.

David says: "A complete and detailed audit will give you the detailed understanding of why your site is not driving the traffic that you think it should. Or why the sales and conversions are not improving in line with your expectations.

"I generally say for any business, a site audit should be a part of a site strategy. The audit should be completed every 12-18 months in full, and should form part of the budget and resources within the organisation.

"For any business, a site audit should be a part of a site strategy."
DAVID SAYCE
@dsayce

"An audit is also a key step before you complete any major changes on the website – such as refreshing or full overhauls.

"As we've seen this year alone, search engines are continually getting smarter. We're seeing more changes in how they work out the search results, and my real tip at the end of this, is not to just rely on that one big audit that you hopefully get round to doing every year/18 months or so.

"Start looking at micro audits. These should really be 5-10 minute overviews looking at the key points on your website. Diving into the key elements of *Google Analytics*, checking those traffic levels, looking at those referrals. Especially those referral spam issues that we've had. And checking things like *Google Search Console*.

"I still see a lot of organisations not diving into the key details and not even browsing their own website as if they were a first-time visitor.

"Dive in, have a run through, do the full customer journey. Understand what it is they're experiencing as they go through the website. And don't forget, there's a lot of tools out there that can give you some really quick, useful information.

"Tools such as *SEM Rush*, whether it's the free or the paid version can give you some real good insight. *GT Metrics* and *Google Page Insights* can help with speed and other issues on the website.

"I think it is vital, whether it is the quickest in-house audit or the larger outsourced version, it should always be seen as an investment."

93) Combine server log and crawl data – Andy Halliday

Andy Halliday, Founder of *Indago Media* feels that there is a lot of value in combining data from different sources.

Andy says: "Instead of doing good technical audits, do great technical audits by combing both server log data and crawl data. The weaknesses of once is covered by the other. I've had some great success in 2016 combining the two together."

So don't necessarily rely on just the one source of data. It's just a case of digging deeper to make sure you have the most reliable source or combination of sources from which to make your decisions.

> *"Do great technical audits by combing both*
> *server log data and crawl data."*
> **ANDY HALLIDAY**
> *@AHalliday*

94) Use the Facebook pixel for free insights – Damon Gochneaur

For Damon Gochneaur, Founder at *Aspiro*, a source of really useful insight is using the *Facebook* pixel.

Damon says: "I am still shocked at the number of businesses not taking advantage of the free insights that Facebook gives us through *Audience Insights*, and the ways that different businesses aren't using that across the different audiences they have.

"With every new client we take on, the first thing we ask them to do – and my number one actionable tip for all businesses – is make sure you have the *Facebook* pixel on every asset you can pixel.

> *"Make sure you have the Facebook pixel on*
> *every asset you can pixel"*
> **DAMON GOCHNEAUR**
> *@DamonGochneaur*

"This means you can start creating custom audiences and you can start segmenting audiences, to learn more about them using *Audience Insights*. And discover even smarter ways to target those audiences, even on other channels. So that you can make sure you're speaking to the right audience."

95) Don't get lost in the data – Dr Angela Hausman

Dr Angela Hausman from *Market Maven* appreciates that it's possible to get lost in your data nowadays – there's so much of it and that's perhaps why some marketers choose to ignore it.

Angela says: "As you're looking to understand consumer behaviour, one of the things I'm seeing, which I'm finding really scary, is a number of recent posts in fairly respectable places, complaining that analytics is ruining marketing.

"If you look into that more deeply, what you see is analytics isn't ruining marketing or destroying marketing's ability.

"What is happening is we're using dumb analytics. In other words, we're doing straight core analysis of correlation with variations of correlation analysis that has no theory behind it.

> *"When you look at your data, you have to be looking at it with some theory in mind."*
> **ANGELA HAUSMA**
> *@marketingletter*

"If you're going to take big data in a very unsophisticated way, throw it into regression modelling, see what comes out and think that that's something that's going to help your organisation, you're absolutely wrong.

"Anytime you look at data, the bigger the data, the more likely you are to find correlations. So when you look at your data, you have to be looking at it with some theory in mind. What are you looking for? What do the variables mean in your data set? How are they likely related to each other?

If you don't do that, predictive analytics are just going to give you garbage. If you base your marketing strategy on that, you're going to end up with garbage. My tip for 2017 is to not forget your marketing in your marketing analytics."

96) Don't just look at the numbers, add creativity back in – Ben Tepfer

While Dr Angela Hausman advises on not forgetting your marketing in your marketing analytics, Ben Tepfer from *Adobe* cautions on not losing your creativity in your insight.

Ben says: "A lot of companies are doing a great job at being creative in the things they do, whether it's innovative marketing campaigns, or whether it's creating offers and testing offers.

"But marketing in many companies has gotten far away from the creative side of things. It's become a lot about numbers and segments.

"Of course these are important, but there's a lot we can do with adding creativity back in, working with our designers, influencing the marketing process. That's the kind of content that really stands out when I think about the emails that I get on a daily basis.

There are so many of [these emails] and they are so repetitive. I have no patience for something that isn't personalised and doesn't look good on every device. There's a lot we can do with adding creativity back in.

> *"I have no patience for something that isn't personalised and doesn't look good on every device."*
>
> **BEN TEPFER**
> *@bentepfer*

"There is a lot we can do in terms of the speed to distribute that content. Working with our designers so that when something happens – maybe our site's down, maybe it's something negative, maybe it's something positive like we sell out of an item before we expected – to being able to provide the best content really quickly.

"For 2017, I hope to see a lot of companies bringing creativity into their digital marketing."

Chapter 14: Insight – summary

- Insight doesn't just mean diving in to your own data, it means getting to know as much as possible about your target audience
- There is so much free data available – start with *Google Analytics* and dive in!
- Join up your data from your CRM or your point-of-sale system into *Google Analytics*
- Include regular audits as part of your digital marketing strategy
- Combine server log data and crawl data to conduct better technical audits

- Make sure you have the *Facebook* pixel on every asset you can pixel
- When you look at your data, you have to be looking at it with some theory in mind
- Don't get lost in your data and forget about creativity

15 THINK OUTSIDE THE BOX

Even though it may seem that there aren't enough hours in the day to test all the digital marketing activities that you currently know oesn't mean that you should place your hands over your ears and refuse to hear about new possibilities.

The opportunities that are open to you have changed so much over the last couple of years, and you can be sure that change will continue to occur at a rapid pace.

97) Expand and diversify – Aleyda Solis

Someone who isn't afraid of change is Aleyda Solis, International SEO Consultant and founder of *Orainti*.

Aleyda says: "My tip is about expanding and diversifying your current online marketing actions to include new platforms every year, leaving a certain budget to do so.

"Sometimes testing something that is just starting, or you have seen has worked well in other industries or international markets is something that you should be doing in order to assess new opportunities.

Even if it doesn't work in conjunction with your established goals, it can help you to better understand your audience behaviour.

> *"I tested Snapchat this year, and for 2017 I'll be creating a messenger bot."*
> **ALEYDA SOLIS**
> *@aleyda*

"I do this myself too. I tested Snapchat this year, and for 2017 I'll be creating a messenger bot, for which there are platforms that allow to develop them without the need to be able to code. Examples of such platforms are *ChatFuel.com*, *ManyChat.com* and *Botsify.com*.

98) Chat apps will be an important CRM opportunity – Purna Virji

For Purna Virji, Senior Ads Training Manager at *Bing*, chat apps are a big opportunity.

Purna says: "I think in 2017 we're going to see an increase in the number of conversational interfaces.

"This does encompass a few different things. The first one is messaging. Text messaging (SMS) is a really huge opportunity that I think we're going to get more and more of here in the West.

"It's been pretty big in China already with *WeChat*. Here we see things like *Kik*, and early adopters like *Sephora* using chatbots to try to have these SMS conversations.

"This area's really big to think about, because most of these messaging apps have more active monthly users than the top four social media accounts. That's a bit bananas to think about! And they're only a few years old!

"Most of these messaging apps have more active monthly users than the top four social media accounts."

PURNA VIRJI
@purnavirji

"They're like the babies of the technology world. And they're still taking over. Two and a half billion active users this year. Predicted to go to 3.6 billion next year. That's pretty big. That's more than the population of India and China put together and then some!

"My grandmother may not have *Facebook*, but she's definitely going to be messaging me on *WhatsApp* or on SMS.

"I think that's going to be quite interesting to think about. We engage with text messaging. We probably would check a message that came to us within five minutes of receiving it. And we're more likely to respond quite quickly.

"They're a really great way for customer relationship management and also for acquisition. *Sephora* is a great example. They have a chatbot that you can send messages to like 'I want makeup tips', or 'I want some product reviews', and those bots talk you through it, as if you were talking to a person.

"This is something big I think we're going to just see more and more of. The other one, the other side of the conversation, is the digital personal assistants, and interacting with them. That's going to grow more and more too.

"We're going to see these personal assistants getting used a lot more. And curating content for us. Advertisers are going to ask 'how can we break through? How can we be found by these digital personal assistants?' It's about aligning with these bots."

A lot to think about there from Purna. So in the future it looks like you're going to be optimising your content for chatbots as well as search engines and humans.

99) Intelligent personal assistants – Jono Alderson

Jono Alderson from *JonoAlderson.com* believes that it's important to get early mover advantage into the emerging world of intelligent personal assistants.

Jono says: "Things like, *Google Home* and *Alexa*, which at the moment are gimmicks, but at any minute now are going to become really serious as consumer behaviour changes.

"People who get there will win big. Specifically it's worth understanding that all of the big brands are fighting to get in these IPA [Intelligent Personal Assistant] devices form *Google*, *Amazon* and *Apple*.

"They are all competing for your living room and your attention. They want to make it really easy to shop and buy in their eco system.

> *"Market much higher up the funnel – understand that you need to create relevance and ownership of the consumer's needs before you sell."*

JONO ALDERSON
@jonoalderson

"The big thing that changes the way that we need to market, and the key tip to take away is to understand that they will start making decisions for consumers. When you want a pizza, they'll decide where it comes from.

"If your washing machine breaks down, they'll decide which one is replacing it. The data they will use to make that decision is going to be largely informed by your own behaviour. What consumers have done in the past will decide how these machines make these decisions.

"As marketers, we need to be marketing much higher up the funnel. Rather than waiting for the consumer to need a 'thing' and be at the point of purchase, we need to be at data points and engagement, six months before that.

"The brands that understand that they need to build a

relationship with me now, in six months will be able to sell me a washing machine without me being involved in that decision.

"So, market much higher up the funnel – understand that you need to create relevance and ownership of the consumer's needs before you sell."

100) Expand your focus to include offline – Shelli Walsh

As well as expanding your digital thinking into new technology, Shelli Walsh, Founder at *Shellshock* advises that you should also be expanding your focus to include offline.

Shelli says: "We need to start thinking and getting out of the search box and become more resourceful in finding traffic sources. Digital has come full circle and now it's more about classic marketing than anything else.

> *"The resurgence of print is happening and I believe that users crave a tangible experience with a physical item to read."*
> **SHELLI WALSH**
> **@shelliwalsh**

"Personally, I think that the single most important approach to marketing that any brand can make is to build a database list that they can repeatedly engage and market to.

"Email marketing is the one area I would recommend that

people pay more attention to – and how to build your business using a newsletter.

"Secondly, the resurgence of print is happening and I believe that users crave a tangible experience with a physical item to read.

"Reading online is much more difficult, and I predict a rise in content being delivered in print, and digital campaigns being combined across email, DM and also exclusive printed customer magazines and catalogues.

"I envisage combining offline print content which is delivered and works alongside digital content will offer a richer experience.

"If you think of brands such as *The Great Discontent*, *99U* and *The Alpine Review*, they're all selling online to a very niche audience, and they're shipping highly desirable print magazines that sell out quickly. I really see this as an area of growth, and something that I'm experimenting with at the moment.

"I spoke to a large mailing house and they quoted a case study to me of a large corporate, who are offering an IPO. And their combined DM and email campaign saw 3 times the response rate of the individual campaigns (i.e. just the DM or just the email). I think there's something really interesting to look at there.

"My actionable tip would be to focus on building your email list database, and to do this you can piggyback on existing lists by using other email lists from complimentary services and businesses, so that you can direct their audience straight to yours. And then expand your focus and consider integrating a print experience in your digital campaigns."

101) Consider website acquisitions as a potential source of traffic – Dave Schneider

The final tip in this chapter that's all about thinking outside the box comes from Dave Schneider, Co-Founder at *Ninja Outreach*.

Dave says: "I wanted to be super tactical and try to come up with something I didn't think anybody else would propose. And therefore I'm going to put fourth acquisitions.

"Earlier this year we swallowed a very small blogging site. And after redirecting all the links, all the traffic came our way, it was a really good boost for business.

"We swallowed a very small blogging site, and after redirecting all the links, all the traffic came our way, it was a really good boost for business."
DAVE SCHNEIDER
@ninjaoutreach

"Thinking about it more, it's a really underappreciated strategy. There are a lot of marketplaces out there nowadays, like *Flippa, Empire Flippers, FE International*, where there are some great businesses or websites being sold.

"And you can potentially get them at a very fair price or even a bargain price, if the value of their traffic – which is basically what they're charging you for, their traffic – is worth a lot more for you.

"I really encourage people to look at acquisitions as a potential strategy in 2017. Why in 2017, why now? You could have always done acquisitions, this is nothing new. But it is getting harder and harder every year to get yourself out there, get known, and grow.

"Therefore if you can, find a site or a small business that you can take over, and use that to give you some link juice, some traffic. It can be a great headstart for you.

"I know that at our company we're definitely going to be looking at making some small acquisitions – most small businesses could do that too.

Chapter 15: Think Outside the Box – summary

- Expand and diversify – pick a completely new platform that you can test in 2017 – consider building your own messenger bot
- Ask yourself how you can make your content discoverable by digital personal assistants
- Market much higher up the funnel – understand that you need to create relevance and ownership of the consumer's needs before you sell
- The resurgence of print is happening – consider what you can do to combine the power of your online and offline marketing mix
- Research to see if there are any websites in your industry sector that you could purchase – relevant

redirects done the right way can be an excellent source of traffic

16 FOCUS

You've come through 15 different chapters so far – the majority of them jam-packed with actionable digital marketing tips.

But how do you ensure that you follow-through and get things done? Should you try to implement as many of these digital marketing opportunities as possible?

102) Be unique in what you do, and focus on doing one thing really well – Jeff Sauer

For Jeff Sauer from *Jeffalytics.com* you should just focus on doing one thing really well.

Jeff says: "My advice is to be unique, because there are a lot of things that are going on. There's a lot of things you could do. Be unique in what you do.

"You don't have to choose every single one of the topics you've learned in this book. In fact you should probably just choose one or two of them, or a few of them, and do them very well.

> *"Instead of being overwhelmed by thinking you need to do 100 things, you should be empowered by saying, 'I can do this one thing, or these two things extremely well.'"*
> **JEFF SAUER**
> *@jeffsauer*

"Being unique in the marketplace is what I would focus on. Where can you be unique? Can you do live video like this event?

"This broadcast is super unique, there's nothing like it that I've seen before so it's really cool to do that. What sets you apart, what's the angle you're going to take?

"Instead of being overwhelmed by thinking you need to do 100 things, you should be empowered by saying, I can do this one thing, or these two things extremely well. Be in a unique position and be the unique player in the marketplace.

"Focus on being unique in one area and do that well and you're going to get a lot more dividends then doing 100 things not very well at all."

103) Focus on what makes a difference – Chris Green

Chris Green, Head of Search at *StrategicIQ* agrees wholeheartedly with the 'focus message'.

Chris says: "Do less of what doesn't work, and more of what does. Stop spending time on the tweaks and tiny fixes, hoping to over-optimise something and get it working. Focus on those elements that do bring home the bacon.

"If you're tweaking title tags or meta descriptions and you have no link profile and you're not getting anywhere it's probably because you've taken your eye off the ball.

"Marketing and optimisation is often an iterative process, but people can often kill that by not staying the course."
CHRIS GREEN
@chrisgreen87

"Only pick the tools you need, stop tweaking and look at the larger picture. But the main thing is, be confident in your overall strategy – and don't be afraid to try and see it through.

"Marketing and optimisation is often an iterative process, but people can often kill that by not staying the course or having the confidence to see it through.

"Invest that time and make friends with journalists, editors and people in that space that you really need help from.

"A lot of people are reluctant to do that as it takes a lot of time and investment, but it always pays off in my experience. Make sure your first interaction with them is not asking for a link – find some other way in to break the ice."

104) Simplify and focus – Jeff Wenberg

The message of simplification and greater focus is something that Jeff Wenberg, Group Coaching Manager at *LeadPages* is encouraging his clients to do.

Jeff says: "For 2017 I would love to see everybody simplify and focus. Typically it is recommended to subscribe to other people's email lists to figure out what the competition is doing.

"But I find that that actually causes a lot more stress and paralyses people from getting stuff done and taking action.

"my simple down-and-dirty tip is to simplify and focus."

JEFF WENBERG
@JeffWenberg

"What I started encouraging people in my groups at *LeadPages* to do if something captures their interest is to make a note – don't ignore it – but after that, put it aside so you can focus on whatever it is you're doing.

"From that moment they started seeing better results. So my simple down-and-dirty tip is to simplify and focus."

105) Find clarity in what you're doing – Stephen Christopher

And for Stephen Christoper from *Seequs*, it's not just about laser targeting of your off-site marketing activities. It's

y

lo, and focus on doing one

ifference – and then stay the
to see it through

our interest, make a note –
fter that, put it aside so you
er it is that you should be

ty to your website – have no
of 3 calls-to-action on your

measure your businesses'
reliably

et a timer. Set constraints for

bringing that whole process of simplification into your website experience.

Stephen says: "Peoples' attention spans are continuing to decrease, so my biggest tip for 2017 is to simplify.

"Find clarity in what you're doing and make sure that it is a very easy message for visitors to your and your clients' websites, telling them what they're supposed to do.

"I see so many websites that have 5 calls-to-action – and people get lost. They're not sure what to read, so they don't read anything. There are 15 social media icons and they don't know where to go.

"Get focused on what your objectives are – we tell our clients to pick the top 1-3 objectives of their website and then make sure that that is all that is shown – especially on your home page.

"Then if the website visitor wants additional information, they can take steps to get deeper into the website. If we give people too many options they'll end up doing nothing.

For the most part, our websites are designed to convert visitors into some form of business.

"I see clients trying to be everything on every social media platform – just pick 1 or 2 that you're really great at and stick with it"
STEPHEN CHRISTOPHER
@StephenMChris

"The second piece of advice that relates to this is social media. Not all of us have as much time, drive or hustle as Gary Vaynerchuk.

"I see clients trying to be everything to everybody on every social media platform. Just pick 1 or 2 platforms that you're really great at and stick with it. Do it consistently, and it will make a much bigger difference on the outcome of your site and online presence."

106) Set and track KPIs – Alex Tachalova

Alex Tachalova, Founder of *DigitalOlympus.net* says that being focused on setting and tracking Key Performance Indicators (KPIs) is key.

Alex says: "For me it's all about KPIs. If you want to be really successful, when you are setting up your KPIs, you need to know how to measure them precisely.

"The problem comes when you are implementing those KPIs and then you discover that you don't know how to measure them – and that's a real problem.

> *"Before you use any metrics to benchmark your success, just be sure that you know how to measure them"*
> **ALEX TACHALOVA**
> *@AlexTachalova*

"Before you use any metrics to benchmark your success, just be sure that you know how to measure them, and you

Chapter 16: Focus – sum

- Be unique in what y
  thing really well
- Focus on what make
  course: don't be af
- If something captur
  don't ignore it – k
  can focus on wh
  doing
- Bring that focus and
  more than a maxin
  website
- Know precisely how
  KPIs consistently a
- Whatever you're doing
  each of your activit

have an environment where you can easily track them."

107) Use a timer – Ed Dale

But it's rather easy to lose focus. And Ed Dale from *Ed Dale.co* has some advice to help us keep doing what we should be doing.

Ed says: "My very simple tip for 2017 is 'use a timer'.

"We live in a world where we don't have a lot of constraints. It may seem like we have a lot of constraints in terms of time etc., but when it comes to implementing any of the hundreds of tips you've heard on this broadcast, putting the constraint of time around things is one of the most powerful tips I can give.

"this broadcast is a living, breathing example of my best tip for 2017."

ED DALE
@Ed_Dale

"If you're doing copywriting, set a timer for 25 minutes, if you're doing a free writing session, set a timer for 10 minutes. If you're doing a script, set a timer.

"In fact, this entire broadcast has been an example of the power of constraint. We've got two minutes to give our best idea for 2017. I think this broadcast is a living, breathing example of my best tip for 2017."

Chapter 16: Focus – summary

- Be unique in what you do, and focus on doing one thing really well
- Focus on what makes a difference – and then stay the course: don't be afraid to see it through
- If something captures your interest, make a note – don't ignore it – but after that, put it aside so you can focus on whatever it is that you should be doing
- Bring that focus and clarity to your website – have no more than a maximum of 3 calls-to-action on your website
- Know precisely how to measure your businesses' KPIs consistently and reliably
- Whatever you're doing, set a timer. Set constraints for each of your activities

17 FINAL THOUGHTS

So many great ideas. So little time.

The challenge with reading a book like this is that it only provides you with a starting point. You're the one who has to decide on the final direction. You're the one who has to choose what you do, and what you don't do.

That's the tough part. But now you need to decide. Did you know that the word 'decide' literally means 'to cut off from'?

What you have just read is specific ideas for your marketing activities for 2017 from some of the world's leading digital marketing authorities.

As Rand Fishkin [a previous *Digital Marketing Radio* guest – check out *DigitalMarketingRadio.com/rand-fishkin*] said in his September 2013 blog post on *Moz.com*, a T-shaped marketer is the kind of marketer that you should consider trying to be. And that still seems to make sense in 2017.

As Rand said: "T-Shaped basically refers to having a light level of knowledge in a broad array of skills, and deep knowledge/ability in a single one (or a few)."

What Rand and a few marketers before him were suggesting is that as marketers, we should be broadly aware of the basics of many different types of marketing activities. And have an in-depth knowledge of one area.

Bearing this in mind, I think that this book has given you the opportunity to be aware of the broad section of marketing opportunities for 2017, helping you manage areas that you're not an expert in.

Hopefully, even if you're not particularly technically capable, you've managed to read through this whole book – including chapters two and three.

I was a little bit wary of sharing such technical tips with you. But the reality is, if you're serious about digital marketing, becoming a great T-shaped marketer means that you need to try to understand the basics of everything that supports whatever you focus on, on a day-to-day basis.

And it's great to challenge yourself! I'm sure you're well aware that digital marketing is constantly evolving, and that means constantly keeping up with things.

So which of the tips resonated with you the most? Add my handle (@DavidBain) to your thoughts on *Twitter* or tag the *Digital Marketing Radio* Facebook page when sharing your thoughts. It really would be wonderful to hear what struck a chord with you.

For me, what Mark Asquith had to say hit the nail on the head. Mark said: "Everyone talks about content marketing, but clients generally only do the content bit."

Personally, I love the content creation process. Especially podcasting.

We tend to think that if our content is good enough it will get shared naturally and we needn't concern ourselves with the content promotion side of things. That's just not true.

You have to promote your content to give it the best possible chance to 'be discovered'. This is what Amy Schmittauer had to say. She publishes on *YouTube* yet she spends a great deal of time on *Facebook Live*, telling her audience on *Facebook* about her *YouTube* content.

If this is what the industry leaders are doing to win at the content game, what makes you think that you can achieve the same results while putting in less effort?!

Something else that I loved hearing – and completely concur with is the focus on understanding people more. With a chapter called 'Think Human' and another one called 'Real People Skills' there wasn't any shortage of advice on really getting to know who your customers are and not hiding behind technology.

As Emeric Ernoult put it: "Too many marketers stay in their ivory tower thinking about marketing strategies, tools, tactics and the latest object on the marketing field."

I also loved what Michael Bonfils had to say – "Focus on behaviour and psychology in order to classify your personas for better content-based attribution channels."

It's the marketers who have the ability to straddle real people understanding with technical know-how that will give themselves the best chance of success in 2017.

Digital marketing in 2017 is about understanding and applying real business skills. It stopped being about trickery and beating the system a long time ago.

Something else that really struck a chord for me was Shelli Walsh's research showing that some people saw three times the response rate by combining direct mail with email campaigns. Shelli's closing advice was to "expand your focus and consider integrating a print experience in your digital campaigns."

That's exactly what I'm trying to do with this book. I would imagine that I'll get more podcast listeners as a result of people reading this book and vice versa. And having a physical book can certainly provide that additional layer of authority.

The last bucket of advice that I'd like to shine a light on are the suggestions to try something that you haven't done before.

And that's probably highlighted best by Aleyda Solis who shared that she's planning on creating her own messenger bot in 2017. As Aleyda explained: "My tip is about expanding and diversifying your current online marketing actions to include new platforms every year."

Purna Virji shared her opinions about chat bots. Purna explained: "I think in 2017 we're going to see an increase in the number of conversational interfaces."

Every year there seems to be a new communications opportunity that launches or becomes mainstream. The question is, which opportunities are right for your business?

The correct strategy seems to be to optimise what you already have, but leave a small amount of time and budget to explore the new arrivals. Just make sure that you're testing platforms that are likely to include your target audience, and that you're communicating on their terms.

But remember chapter 16 – focus. Keep on doing what's right for you and your business. At the beginning of the book I talked about how it might have been possible to treat digital marketing as a single entity ten years ago. Nowadays you just cannot be everywhere. And if you try, it's a recipe for diminishing the quality of what you do, and taking your eye off your core audience.

If you haven't done so already, remember to sign-up for the bonuses that come with this book. Several of the experts involved have been kind enough to provide all readers with valuable extras such as several months' free access to their marketing software. Check out and sign-up for all the free bonuses at *DigitalMarketingRadio.com/Book*.

And while you're on the *DigitalMarketingRadio.com* website, make sure you subscribe to the podcast. I'm going to be interviewing more experts soon – just click on one of the subscription links on the site and new episodes will automatically download to your mobile device, whenever they become available.

I really hope that we can make this a regular occurrence. It would be fab if you could join us for 'Digital Marketing in 2018, 2019, 2020'…

If you found this book to be valuable, I'd really appreciate you taking a couple of minutes of your time to leave a rating and review on Amazon – or wherever you happened to purchase it.

And if you didn't like it at all, my name's Mark Asquith. ;)

As I say at the end of each episode of the *Digital Marketing Radio* podcast… until we meet again, be fantabulous. And do one thing that scares you. Adios.